Practical Economics

To Mohammed Qamar:

With Best Wishes

Nika Gilauri

Practical Economics

Economic Transformation and Government Reform in Georgia 2004–2012

Nika Gilauri
Tbilisi, Georgia

ISBN 978-3-319-45768-0   ISBN 978-3-319-45769-7 (eBook)
DOI 10.1007/978-3-319-45769-7

Library of Congress Control Number: 2016954025

Cover pattern © Melisa Hasan. All rights reserved, used with permission.

Printed on acid-free paper

This Palgrave Macmillan imprint is published by Springer Nature
The registered company is Springer International Publishing AG
The registered company address is: Gewerbestrasse 11, 6330 Cham, Switzerland

To Maiko, Mari & Zuka

PREFACE

In 2003, Georgia was a broken country: riddled with corruption, devoid of natural resources, and in economic decline. Nine years later, Georgia was a driver of change and renewal in the region. The economy was growing fast, international investors responded well to Georgia's business-friendly environment, Transparency International acknowledged the successful fight against corruption, and the World Bank had proclaimed Georgia the world's top reformer for the period from 2006 to 2011.

What happened? After the Rose Revolution in 2003, a new generation of leaders took charge. Following a rigorous "less is more" approach, the new government cut regulation and bureaucracy down to size. The number of taxes was slashed from 21 to 6, while tax revenue as a percentage of GDP soared from 7 to 24 percent. In parallel, the government invested in critical infrastructure and one-stop public services to attract foreign investment and encourage private enterprise. In a nutshell, Georgia went for growth and implemented a plethora of radical reforms in parallel tracks.

What happened in Georgia between 2004 and 2012 is one of only a handful of examples of true transformation on a national scale in the twenty-first century, and perhaps the most comprehensive case. Between 2006 and 2011 alone, Georgia successfully completed 35 reforms qualifying under the World Bank's "Doing Business" criteria, i.e., half a dozen per year. According to the World Bank's "Ease of Doing Business" report, the global average for such reforms was 1.7 per year at the time. What is more, all Georgian reforms were initiated and overseen by the same small group of people, rather than by different consecutive administrations. "Since the World Bank began keeping records, no other country has made so many deep reforms in so many different areas so consistently."[1] Of course, not all Georgian reforms were 100 percent successful. A few of them failed, and others could not be finalized, at least for the time being, for political, economic, or social reasons. But the vast majority of the reforms were success stories that helped transform Georgia from a failed state into a fast-growing economy with great prospects.

Drawing on my experience in Georgia, I currently advise a number of governments around the world and analyze dozens of national economies, and I observe that most of them are facing very similar problems. While developing countries may have the most to learn from Georgia, a surprising number of developed countries share many of their objectives, such as bridling bureaucracy, easing the regulatory burden, and fighting corruption. To my great dismay, many governments are unwilling to learn from one another. As a result, the same mistakes are made over and over again.

Of course, there are significant differences between countries – culture, history, the stage of economic development, the geopolitical situation, the levels of education, and social maturity. But at the same time, there are many things that are the same for almost all countries and their governments. Most of them strive for a higher standard of living, better education, more effective healthcare systems, greater security, economic growth, and lower unemployment rates. And most governments share not only these objectives but the challenges that make it difficult to achieve them as well: tight budgets, increasing levels of debt, corruption, and inefficient public services. So why not learn from one another? There are only so many ways to fund the healthcare system, to collect taxes efficiently, to provide better services to the public, to prepare for a downward economic cycle, or create a business-friendly environment. Don't get me wrong – I'm not advocating a copy-and-paste approach. In practical reality, there are too many differences, big and small, between different countries. All I am saying is that it is worthwhile studying what others have tried, what has worked, what hasn't worked, and drawing the right inferences for one's own situation. According to *the Economist* and its most recently published article in July 2016, Georgia's knowledge and experience in fighting corruption serves as a powerful example and model of how to crusade corruption globally, even in such big countries like Nigeria.[2]

And this is exactly what this book is all about – it is a record of what happened in Georgia between 2004 and 2012. Specifically, I set out to chronicle the reforms that thoroughly transformed Georgia – from one of the most corrupt countries in 2003 to one of the least corrupt countries in

2010; the reforms that took Georgia from 112th place in 2006 to 8th place in 2014 in the World Bank's "Ease of Doing Business" report, that helped quadruple the economy (in nominal terms) within nine years; and the reforms that helped Georgia come out of the 2008/2009 recession faster than any other country in the region despite its lack of natural resources and despite the combined burden of the world financial crisis and the Russian invasion.

This book provides a detailed analysis of the reforms made in Georgia. It starts by discussing why the Georgian case is exemplary for other countries and proceeds to describe the fight against corruption, the rightsizing of government, the creation of a business-friendly environment, tax and customs reform, the privatization of state-owned enterprises, energy sector reforms, and smart spending approaches applied to welfare, healthcare, education, and procurement. In some cases, the description draws on the experiences of other countries, either because they served as an inspiration for Georgia's reforms or because approaches pioneered in Georgia were successfully applied there.

In a nutshell, this book is my attempt to answer one question: how do you manage a transformation to bring about fast and sustainable growth? In what follows, I approach this question from two angles:

- What is the right size for a government, both in terms of its regulatory footprint and in terms of its budget in relation to the size of the economy?
- How do you ensure a government's efficiency in terms of its decision making, its interaction with the private sector, its financial flows, and the services it provides?

The book concludes with a discussion of leadership, in recognition of the fact that even the best approaches would not apply themselves. It takes determined leadership to make them work – the courage to fix what is broken, to try innovative approaches, and to learn from one's mistakes.

So is this a book for leaders only, for heads of state and government? Far from it. I believe there is something here for everyone who takes an interest in public affairs – politicians, civil servants, consultants, and all active citizens who may be interested in how governments function and how they can be transformed. This book also shows that none of the major economic theories stands the test of practical application. Some people believe that the state should redistribute wealth from the rich to the poor. Others believe that the freedom of enterprise is more important. Many believe that a monetarist approach is the best solution to the world's economic problems, while others favor Keynesian economics. In my experience, none of these theories is universally applicable. Every given economic problem requires its own solution. This is why I advocate what I call *Practical Economics*. Practical Economics is about finding the right mix of economic policies for a given country at a given moment. This book is about the mix of economic policies that transformed the Georgian economy between 2004 and 2012. While some of these policies may not be applicable to any other country, I will make the case that many of them are relevant for many countries, developing as well as developed, today.

You never know when you will get a chance to do something good for your country. In my case, it came when I least expected it. I had never worked in politics. I was never the member of any political party, not even when I was prime minister. I was not personally acquainted with any of the political leaders who came into power in 2004 before they asked me to be their minister of energy.[3] And yet I was fortunate enough to get to work side by side with many outstanding people. I was fortunate enough to get to drive and lead many groundbreaking reforms. I was fortunate enough to get a chance to help build a better future for my country. But before I got the call, I would never have imagined that I would get to do any of those things, although I had always wanted to do something for my country, waiting for my moment to come. So when your moment comes, be prepared. I hope this book will help you seize the day.

Carpe diem!

Nika

Notes

1. World Bank (2011); see http://www.ccifg.ge/de/business-in-georgia/why-to-invest-in-georgia/10-reasons-to-invest-in-georgia/ (retrieved in May 2016).
2. http://www.economist.com/blogs/economist-explains/2016/07/economist-explains-13.
3. For the full story, please see Chapter 7, Reforming the Energy Sector.

ACKNOWLEDGMENTS

I gratefully acknowledge the help of my team at Reformatics – Ms. Tamara Kovziridze, Mr. Vakhtang Lejava, Mr. David Koberidze, and Mr. Givi Chanukvadze; the support of the publishing team at Palgrave Macmillan; and the services of my editor Cornelius Grupen, who helped me shape the structure and the style of this book.

Also, special thanks to Neil Janin – who was the first one to read the manuscript and to give suggestions that in the end helped me to structure the book.

Contents

LIST OF FIGURES

CHAPTER 1

Carpe Diem

Abstract This chapter, the introduction to Practical Economics, discusses the challenge of fixing a broken country and describes the situation in Georgia in the early 2000s. The author, Georgia's former prime minister, Nika Gilauri, explains why he believes that other countries can learn from the reforms he oversaw between 2004 and 2012. The chapter contains an overview of the impact of this large-scale transformation in areas ranging from corruption and doing business to economic growth and energy supply, as well as a personal account of how Mr. Gilauri, a political novice at the time, became a member of the cabinet in 2004.

Keywords Practical Economics · Georgia · Prime minister · Nika Gilauri · Doing business · Reforms

As I said, you never know when you will get a chance to do something good for your country. For me, the call of duty came in December 2003, shortly after the Rose Revolution. I didn't recognize the number on my phone's display, but I had a distinct feeling that something important was about to happen. I took the call.

"Hello?"

"Hi, this is David. I am calling from the Prime Minister's Office. He would like to see you."

© The Author(s) 2017
N. Gilauri, *Practical Economics*,
DOI 10.1007/978-3-319-45769-7_1

"When?"

"Right now?"

"Of course. I'm on my way."

I was stunned. I had never met the prime minister. I didn't know any other cabinet members either. I had attended the protests on Rustaveli Avenue the previous month, but I had not met any of the leaders. I really had no idea why the prime minister wanted to see me.

How did his office even get my number? Was it related to my job? I was working in the energy sector at the time, and I had a reputation as a critic of the government's energy policy. Perhaps they had come to me for an insider's perspective? Or had I done something wrong and was about to be reprimanded? But why would the prime minister deal with me personally?

Either way I looked at it, this was big. I hurried to the State Chancellery.

The prime minister was sitting in his office by himself. We exchanged very brief hellos.

"What do you think about the energy sector in Georgia?"

"Excuse me, but how do you even know about me?"

"Irrelevant. Answer my question."

I described some of the challenges I had encountered, but he quickly interrupted me.

"How long do you need to prepare a presentation about the energy sector?"

"Until tomorrow?"

"Tomorrow? That's not possible."

"I already have a presentation. I just need to go over it one more time."

He looked puzzled.

"Did you know that this is why I asked you to come here today?"

"No, but I have been working on improvement ideas for the energy sector for some time."

I wasn't lying. I was so fed up with the blackouts, the mismanagement, and the corruption that I had written down my thoughts on how to make it work. But I had not shown this to anyone.

"Okay, come back the day after tomorrow."

When I went back, the prime minister was not alone. About half a dozen people were gathered at the table, including his chief of staff and the minister of finance. I started my presentation. The prime minister interrupted me with a question, but I asked him to let me continue and save his questions for later. I said this simply because the answer to his question was on my next slide, but the second I had said it, I was afraid I might have been overly brusque. Curiously, everybody present seemed to be impressed with my bold move, especially the prime minister himself.

"I think we have found our man."

He was whispering, but everybody heard him. I went on, but he interrupted me again.

"Will you be my Minister of Energy?"

Now it was my turn to look puzzled.

"Huh?"

"How old are you?"

"28."

"That's very young, but we are a revolutionary government. We have to revolutionize everything. There are opportunities in your life that you should not say no to. So will you be the Minister of Energy of Georgia?"

I mustered all my courage.

"On one condition."

"What's that?"

"I will not cut my hair."

At the time, my hairstyle was not what most Georgian's would have described as ministerial.

"Of course. No problem."

1.1   LEARNING FROM GEORGIA

Why should you read this book, even if you are neither Georgian nor a student of the country and its history? Because the lessons learned in Georgia between 2004 and 2012 are applicable to many other countries, both developing and developed. Here is why:

- In that period, Georgia was the closest thing to a *laboratory for political and economic reform* you will find in real life.
- In that short period, Georgia went through more *political permutations and economic cycles* than many other countries experience in a century.
- Although the transformation happened under unique circumstances, the *challenges* Georgia faced will be familiar to governments in many countries.

Think of this book as a blueprint for successful transformation, and I'm sure you will find something of value in it, wherever you live and whatever your position is.

1.1.1   Laboratory of Reforms

The nine-year period after the Rose Revolution was one of those rare occasions when the vast majority of the population is yearning for change. The new government enjoyed an 80 percent approval rating when it started conducting its reforms. In November 2003, during the Rose Revolution, people had taken to the streets, demanding a new government. When that new government was in place, they demanded fast reforms across the board – political, economic, and social. The major factions in Georgia's society were on the same page – politicians, common people, captains of industry, intellectuals, and even the opposition.

There was broad consensus that change needed to come fast, if it was to come at all. The new government duly adopted what was sometimes referred to as the *Big Bang* approach. We would reform everything, and we would do it quickly. Instead of drafting comprehensive development plans, taking one step at a time, and reviewing progress every step of the way, we went in like the mavericks we were. We decided to do and learn, rather than to sit and wait. We were aware that we would get some things wrong at first, but we were willing to take that risk and prepared to learn from our mistakes.

From the get-go, we were determined to take inspiration from successful reforms in other countries, much the way I encourage the readers of this book to take inspiration from Georgia. We studied what other countries had done in similar situations, where they had succeeded, where they had failed, and what mistakes they had made along the way. We took what worked and adapted it to the new political reality and the specific local requirements in Georgia.

Post-revolution Georgia was the rare case of a country tackling reforms in all areas: fiscal and monetary policies; welfare, healthcare, and education; and public accountability, security, and agriculture. Nothing was left out. What makes this case so rare is the fact that most governments initiate reforms in one or two areas but almost never across the board. This is due to the fact that most societies are not ready to embrace change on this scale. All things considered, we set out to build a modern state – not from scratch but from the ruins left by decades of corruption and neglect – 70 years of Soviet regime; Russian-led wars on the Georgian territory and a civil war in the post-Soviet 1990s; and corrupt and criminal government's rule in late 1990s through early 2000s. The starting position was not the best.

1.1.2 Everything that Could Have Happened, Had Happened

Between 2004 and 2012, Georgia went through more political, social, and geopolitical permutations than most countries see in a century or their entire history: a peaceful revolution; local, parliamentarian, and presidential elections; country-wide protests organized by the opposition that paralyzed the capital city; breaking up the protests and announcing a curfew that eventually led to early presidential elections; dealing with breakaway regions and a Russian invasion; wartime management of supplies and finances; sheltering internally displaced persons; and battling the influence of crime syndicates that had effectively ruled the country for decades. Each stage had its own challenges, and – in most cases – its own success stories, many of which I tell in this book.

Georgia did not only go through all kinds of political change in the period in question, but all major economic cycles as well: economic growth, economic downturn, pre-election economics, and even the economic challenges specific to times of armed conflict. Each of these situations has its own dos and don'ts, and Georgia got it right under pretty much all circumstances. Despite the combined effects of a legacy of debt, the world financial crisis, the Russian invasion, and local political tensions, Georgia came out of the recession quicker than any of its neighbors.[1] Even during the war with Russia in 2008, the economy ran like clockwork. Not even the prices of food products increased. In 2004, we found that not only had the previous government emptied all coffers at the treasury and state-owned entities but the outstanding pensions and salaries for government employees added up to 10 percent of gross domestic product (GDP). We were broker than broke. But in 2012, we handed over positive balance of just under 10 percent of GDP to the incoming government. Debt had decreased to 34.8 percent of GDP, and external reserves had increased by a factor of ten in nominal terms and almost quadrupled as a percent of GDP (Fig. 1.1).

1.1.3   Unique, but Exemplary

There is no debating the fact that the geopolitical circumstances under which we made our reforms were exceptional. The country was in shambles, and its surrounding region was in disarray. At the time, nobody would have bet on Georgia to transform itself from a failed state into a growing democracy over the course of a single decade. And yet it happened. U.S. President George Bush called Georgia a "beacon of democracy" for the region, a part of the world in which free markets and modern institutions were virtually unknown at the time. What is more, we were up against repeated Russian attempts to undermine Georgia's development model and growth path, a string of events that culminated in the 2008 invasion.

At the same time, the challenges Georgia faced along its transformation journey resemble those many other countries struggle with: weak institutions, widespread corruption, inefficiency of the public sector, a low level of economic development, insufficient infrastructure, limited prospects of growth and prosperity, a tainted international image, etc. Many countries try and fail to solve these problems, sometimes over the course of many decades. Georgia solved these problems, and I invite other countries to take advantage of the lessons that we learned along the way.

1.2   Georgia Before and After

Between 2004 and 2012, Georgia was transformed from a failed state that faced bankruptcy into a stable economy with excellent growth prospects. Here is an overview of some of the telltale indicators of this transformation: corruption, ease of doing business, economic growth, and energy supply.

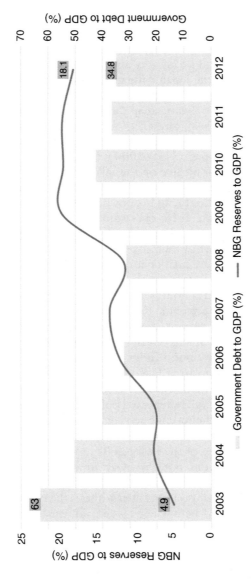

Fig. 1.1 NBG reserves to GDP/government debt to GDP. (*Source:* National Bank of Georgia; Ministry of Finance of Georgia.)

1.2.1 Corruption

In 2003, Transparency International's Global Corruption Index revealed Georgia to be one of the most corrupt countries in the world (ranked 127th out of 133), along with or behind much of Africa and many former Soviet Union countries, and a long way away from "clean" countries such as the United States, Canada, Japan, Singapore, South Korea, and much of Western Europe. Georgia was on par with Angola and behind Zimbabwe and Republic of Congo.[2] Even small businesses needed "krishas," a Russian term that describes a "caretaker" who is well connected with the government, to survive. To get a job as a police officer that paid USD 20 per month, you had to pay a USD 2000 bribe. It was still a worthwhile investment because you didn't live on the salary but rather on the bribes. Traffic police officers would actually pay bribes to their superiors to have additional traffic signs and traffic lights put up – not to improve safety on the streets, but to increase their opportunities to take bribes. In the *Corruption Barometer* survey, about 80 percent of Georgians said that corruption was a major part of their lives.

In 2010, Transparency International conducted a similar survey, asking nationals of 183 different countries whether they, or a member of their family, had paid a bribe in the past 12 months. Only 4 percent of Georgians said that they had, compared with 5 percent in the European Union (average) and the United States. Georgia was outranked only by a handful of countries, including the United Kingdom, Canada, Singapore, and New Zealand.

In the 2012 Global Corruption Index, Georgia was ranked 51st out of 174 countries, ahead of many EU countries such as Czech Republic, Slovakia, Latvia, and just behind South Korea.[3] According to the 2012 *Corruption Barometer*, Georgians reported only very few cases of corruption (none when dealing with the revenue service, 2 percent when dealing with utilities, 4 percent when dealing with the police, and 5 percent when dealing with the court system), one of the best results in the world. To make this happen, the government did not shy away from radical measures. For example, the entire traffic police force (16,000 employees) was fired in one day, in July 2004, and traffic was much safer without the traffic police on the streets. They were replaced with a new, well-paid, much smaller force of about 2500 officers. If they were caught taking a bribe, they went to prison. Before, police officers had been hiding behind corners to demand a bribe as soon as a driver ran a red light. After the cleanup, officers were out in the open, warning drivers not to run a red light or turn right where it wasn't allowed. This goes to show that innate corruption does not exist. Corruption is a disease. Every nation wants to get rid of it. If the time is right, and all forces in society pull together, it can be eradicated in a very short period of time. If there were such a thing as innate or cultural corruption, Georgia would still be as corrupt a country as it was just a decade ago.

1.2.2   Ease of Doing Business

In 2006, Georgia ranked 112th in the World Bank's "Ease of Doing Business" report, just behind Nigeria and Kyrgyzstan. At the time, BP was the only foreign investor, and even this was just because the pipeline the company was building (from Baku in Azerbaijan to Ceyhan in Turkey) passed through Georgia.

In 2012, Georgia was the only developing country that made the top ten of the World Bank's "Ease of Doing Business 2013" report, as well as the only country to make the jump from a rank below 100th place to the top ten, reaching 8th place, just behind the United Kingdom and Denmark, and ahead of Germany and South Korea. Georgia was number one worldwide in the "registering property" category, third in "dealing with construction permits," fourth in "getting credit," and seventh in "starting a business." In 2011, the World Bank proclaimed Georgia the world's top reformer for the period 2006 to 2011 (Figs. 1.2 and 1.3).

1.2.3   Economic Growth

In 2003, Georgia was widely regarded as one of the least developed countries in the World. GDP per capita was only USD 922. The government's budget revenues were less than 7 percent of GDP, although taxes were higher than in any other country in the region. The unemployment rate was 17 percent. Growth prospects were grim, given the very limited natural resources and low level of foreign direct investment.

By 2012, Georgia had quadrupled its economy in nominal terms and doubled its GDP per capita in terms of purchasing power parity (PPP). So far, it is among only a handful of non-oil exporting countries to have achieved such growth in the twenty-first century. According to my research, only 18 non-oil exporting countries have managed to double their GDP per capita in terms of PPP in any given decade since 1980 – Singapore, Hong Kong, South Korea, Ireland, China, Latvia, Lithuania, and some other former members of the Soviet Union. Georgia did it

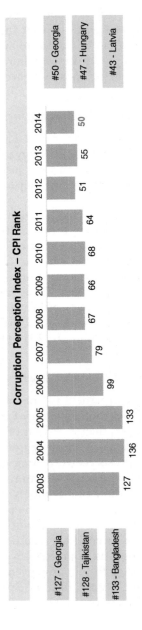

Fig. 1.2 Georgia in international rankings: Corruption Perception Index. (*Source:* TI "Corruption Perception Index Reports.")

Fig. 1.3 Georgia in international rankings: Ease of Doing Business rank. (*Source:* World Bank Group, Ease of Doing Business reports.)

consistently in all decades ending between 2006 and 2012, i.e., GDP per capita in terms of PPP in every one of those years was twice what it had been ten years before – 2006 vs. 1996, 2007 vs. 1997, and so on, through 2012 vs. 2002. Georgia's achievement is even more remarkable in light of the worldwide financial crisis that broke out in 2007 and the military invasion by Russia in 2008.

Not only has the Georgian economy grown at an average rate of 6.7 percent between 2003 and 2012, one of the highest growth rates among countries worldwide that do not produce oil, it also was the fastest country in its region to come out of the recession that was triggered by the world financial crisis (Figs. 1.4 and 1.5).

1.2.4   Energy Supply

In early 2000s, Georgia suffered from the worst power shortage in the region. The Ministry of Energy itself was without electricity. During the winter months, the country's utilities delivered electricity only for two hours per day. People took to the streets, demanding to know when exactly they would get their two hours. They had long given up hope of 24-hour electricity supply. In the evenings, you could actually hear people shouting "hurray" every time that electricity supply was restored. At the same time, stealing electricity was a national sport. One of the more innovative techniques that some customers used to cheat distribution companies was a sensor-based remote control that switched on the meter when an inspector came within a four-meter radius of the meter (from beyond four meters it was impossible to see whether a meter was running or not).

By 2007, less than three years after the new government had taken office, not only did Georgia enjoy 24-hour electricity supply but it had also become a net electricity exporter, supplying electricity to all neighboring countries. Total distribution losses (including commercial and technical losses in the distribution network) decreased from more than 60 percent to less than 8 percent (Fig. 1.6).

1.3   ROOM FOR IMPROVEMENT

If the transformation was such a success story, why did Georgia's ruling party lose the elections in October 2012? Was it because the reforms went too far? No. In fact, the opposite is true. It was because the reforms didn't go far enough.

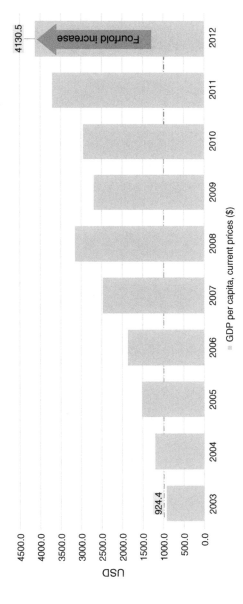

Fig. 1.4 GDP per capita. (*Source:* IMF.)

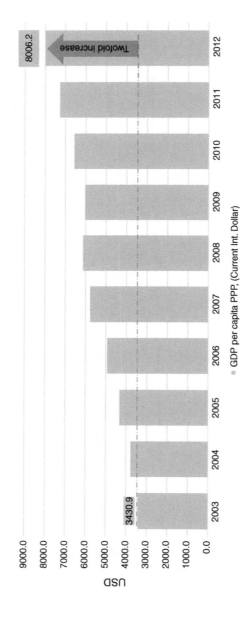

Fig. 1.5 GDP per capita PPP. (*Source:* IMF.)

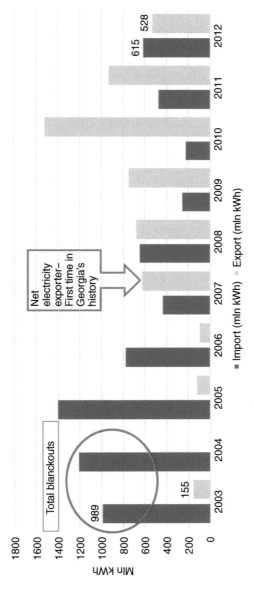

Fig. 1.6 Electricity export and import. (*Source:* Ministry of Energy of Georgia.)

The biggest mistake the government made was not to reform the justice system in time. Even though some changes were introduced, the pace was slow and the results were barely visible. For example, in 2010, 98 percent of all cases, both criminal and civil, were settled in favor of the prosecutor's office. The prosecutor's office in some cases abused its powers, especially when dealing with local businesses. This was a period when businesses were learning to pay taxes. In majority of cases, the deals made by prosecutor's office were understandable – there were clear cases of tax evasions, but as it appeared there were cases where the approach was excessively harsh and by far not fair. As a result, people got frustrated with the inappropriate conduct of the prosecutor's office.

Defenders of the harsh approach say that this was the only way to break the overpowering influence of crime families, bring the crime rate down, and root out corruption. They are right, and in fact, many citizens initially accepted the hardline approach as necessary. Severe diseases call for severe treatment. Centralizing power and showing no mercy were the right remedies during the first five years after the Rose Revolution. But by 2010, the rule of corruption and crime had been broken. The mentality of the population had changed. Before 2004, crime and corruption had been the norm. When you asked teenagers what they wanted to grow up to be, most of them said that they dreamed of becoming a "thief in law," a local expression referring to the head of a crime family. But only a few years later, most teenagers said that they wanted to become a police officers or businesspeople, according to a survey conducted in 2010.

Once these results had been achieved, however, the justice system should have been thoroughly reformed. But this reform never came. As a result, citizens felt that they were being treated unfairly by the government. This frustration set in motion a course of events that eventually led to the defeat of the ruling party in the 2012 elections. In *Getting Georgia Right*, Svante Cornell puts it this way: The government of Georgia "found that to build the state, they [government] had to centralize power and exert stronger control over society and moribund state institutions. A functioning state is a prerequisite for liberal and constitutional democracy, rather than the other way around. Especially for a country subjected to the type of external pressure that Georgia has been, it would be utopian to believe that a liberal democracy could develop without the framework of a sovereign and functioning state. Thus, the priority accorded to state-building was understandable. The problem in Georgia was that the revolutionaries [...] failed in some areas to halt the practice – perhaps necessary in the early years – of cutting corners in terms of due process and the rule of law."[4]

Failing to reform the justice system was not the only reason the ruling party was defeated in the 2012 elections. Another reason was that the ruling team started to believe that it was unbeatable. It had performed nothing short of an economic miracle, after all. Thousands of corrupt and underperforming civil servants had been fired. Despite these and many other initially unpopular reforms, the ruling party had won numerous local, presidential, and parliamentary elections. It had survived the Russian invasion and a coup staged by an oligarch.[5] It could simply not imagine losing an election to anyone. In fact, some people still struggle to accept the fact that they lost in 2012. This sense of invincibility weakened the team. If you think that your team is immune to outside challengers, unhealthy internal competition will arise, and your political radar will invariably deteriorate.

So it's not for a lack of success of its reforms that the ruling party was defeated. It was defeated because the reforms did not go far enough, and because the many successes instigated an unhealthy sense of complacency in the top team. I encourage the readers of this book to take inspiration from Georgia's successes and learn from its mistakes. To this date, our reform agenda was the most comprehensive and – all things considered – most successful of such efforts in the twenty-first century.

NOTES

1. The only year of economic decline was 2009 (–3.9 percent). By 2010, the economy was growing again – at a rate of 6.4 percent. The average growth rate between 2003 and 2012 was 6.7 percent. See subsequent chapters for details.

2. Georgia was on par with Angola, Cameroon, Tajikistan, and Azerbaijan, behind Libya (118th), Sierra Leone, the Republic of Congo (joint 113th), and Zimbabwe (112th). The only countries that were ranked below Georgia were Myanmar, Paraguay, Haiti, Nigeria, and Bangladesh (*Transparency International Report* for 2003).

3. In 2012, Georgia ranked 51st, ahead of many EU countries, such as the Czech Republic, Latvia (joint 54th), Croatia, Slovakia (both 62nd), Romania (66th), Italy (72nd), and Bulgaria (75th), and just behind South Korea and Lithuania (*Transparency International Report* for 2012).

4. http://www.martenscentre.eu/sites/default/files/publication-files/get ting_georgia_right_-_website.pdf (retrieved in May 2016).

5. http://www.independent.co.uk/news/uk/home-news/georgian-billionaire-declared-enemy-of-the-state-is-found-dead-in-surrey-exile-782016.html (retrieved in May 2016).

CHAPTER 2

Fighting Corruption

Abstract This chapter describes the measures taken in Georgia after the 2004 to fight corruption, eradicate the shadow economy, and promote economic growth. Examples of such measures include better pay for public officials, performance rewards, deregulation, simplification of regulation, and investments in checks and balances. Based on his experience leading successful anti-corruption reforms, the author challenges the widespread belief that corruption is innate in societies and provides both concrete examples of creative corruption-prevention approaches, such as mystery shopping, and evidence of the impact of his reforms in Georgia, such as the country's performance in Transparency International's Corruption Perception Index and the Global Corruption Barometer.

Keywords Urgency · Administration · Meritocracy · Bureaucrats · Laffer curve · Procurement · Electronic · Transparent · Tender · Auction

When the new government was approved in the winter of 2004, Georgia was falling apart economically. GDP per capita was at the level of third-world countries like Togo or Malawi. Almost half the population was either unemployed or earning only a few dollars a month. But more importantly, the country was running dramatically low on trust. If we wanted to save Georgia, we would have to make the government and its agents accountable for their actions. Public officials would have to start playing by the rules, and those who didn't would have to be brought to justice. We wanted Georgians to trust their leaders, and foreign investors to trust the Georgian economy as a whole. Fighting corruption was the key to both of these goals.

2.1   DON'T WASTE A CRISIS

I refuse to believe that corruption is innate in any person or society. Corruption results from poor choices, and it is the main obstacle for any country to grow. Some countries may grow despite high levels of corruption, usually fueled by natural resources. But such growth is not sustainable, and it doesn't create a middle class capable of serving as the backbone of a stable society, unless substantial reforms are conducted in time.

Until 2004, Georgia had been in the hands of leaders who accepted corruption as a lesser evil. But in 2003, the Rose Revolution changed the game. The crisis engendered an unprecedented willingness to change, as well as a sense of urgency shared by everyone. The vast majority of the population was fed up with being cheated out of their own country by the ruling elite and its accomplices. An approval rate of 80 percent for the new government and its reform program gave us a clear mandate to clean up the country. This mandate cut across all levels of society and all political parties, and we were determined not to let this rare opportunity go to waste. And while Georgia today is far from flawless, few would deny that it is in an infinitely better place than Georgia in 2003. Paradoxically, it was the crisis that helped us do it. Without the crisis, we would never have been able to turn things around in Georgia. When I look back now, I see the crisis as a blessing in disguise, despite all the hardship that it brought about.

The reforms we implemented to fight corruption in Georgia produced fast results. In a 2003 survey conducted by Transparency International, more than two-thirds of the respondents (67 percent) had said they expected the level of corruption to increase, or stay at the same level, within the next three years. Only one year later, that figure was down to 11 percent. The vast majority of the population had obviously regained trust in the government's ability to return the country to a state of compliance and accountability. In 2007, independent observers recognized that the post-revolution government had "done better than any [of its] predecessors at battling corruption" (NYT 2007).[1]

While many of the changes the government made were specific to the situation in Georgia at the time, our fight against corruption rested on three pillars that I consider relevant for any country that is serious about cleaning up its act: the right *incentives* for government employees, *simplification* of rules and regulations, and the *enforcement* of the rules without exemptions. Additionally, I have also come to believe and will demonstrate that *regulatory restraint* is the best long-term precaution against the resurgence of corruption. By regulatory restraint I mean a degree of regulation that maximizes growth and reflects the capacity of a government to enforce the rules it makes. This degree varies with a given country's economic performance and administrative capability.

2.2 Incentives: Carrots and Sticks

Before 2003, the salaries for government officials were so ridiculously low that nobody expected them to work without bribes.[2] To end the rule of bribery, the new government took a three-step approach.

Step one was to replace most high-ranking officials with a cohort of young, inexperienced, but highly motivated and hard-working people with no track record of corruption. If in doubt, we picked the candidate with a clean record over the tenured professional who might have been entangled in the corrupt practices that we were trying to put an end to. The majority of pre-revolution officials had spent their lives working for the Soviet government. This generation of politicians and administrators was not only accustomed to corrupt practices, their entire political value system was based on the belief that stealing from the government residing in far-away Moscow was a good thing. Unfortunately, this mentality did not change when the Soviet Union unraveled. So the post-revolution government really had no choice but to let the old guard go and run with a new generation of highly motivated, inexperienced people (Fig. 2.1).

Admittedly, this was not a perfect solution. A lot of relevant experience was lost, and not all new hires were not up to their jobs, but this was the price we had to pay if we wanted to start with a relatively clean slate. Of course, there was no guarantee that the newcomers would always play by the rules, but there was a much better chance that they would than for experienced corrupt officials to come clean. By and large, our plan worked out.

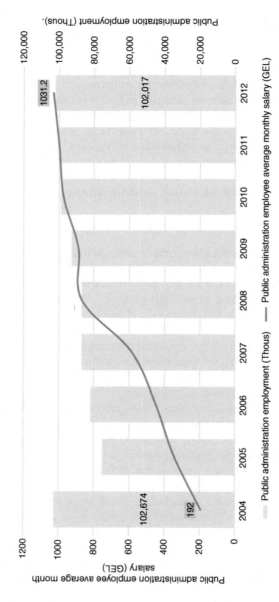

Fig. 2.1 Public administration employment and average monthly salaries. (*Source:* National Statistics Office of Georgia; Ministry of Finance of Georgia.)

Step two was to increase salaries to make sure public servants would not have to revert to corrupt practices to feed their families. A minister's monthly salary increased from about USD 75 in 2003 to USD 1200 in 2004, and it increased further in later years. In some cases, average salaries for working-level administrators and members of the traffic police force increased by a factor of ten, from about USD 20 to USD 200. These increases were financed by a significant increase in tax revenues, which I will discuss in the next chapter, and by the eradication of corruption itself. Government officials would not get rich under the new regime, but nobody would have to take bribes to feed their family any longer. In effect, corrupt officials lost the moral high ground. This was an important step on the way to a law-abiding society.

Step three was to infuse public service with a spirit of meritocracy. We introduced a bonus system that rewarded both institutional compliance and personal performance. At the same time, we made it abundantly clear that violators would be punished swiftly and severely. In other words, we promised carrots to those who were willing to build a better Georgia, and we made sure we had the sticks we needed to crack down on corruption.

2.3   SIMPLIFICATION: THE DEVIL IS IN THE DETAILS, UNLESS THE DETAILS ARE SIMPLE

Before 2004, the tax system was so complicated and the total tax burden was so high, especially considering the very low level of economic development of the country, that it was widely accepted that no company could pay all of the taxes levied on it and stay in business. A company's tax burden depended on who the tax collector was, what kind of bribe the company offered, and how fierce the competition was in a given industry or region. Bribing the tax collector was the only way to stay in business. With the introduction of the new tax code, the number of taxes was reduced from 21 to 6; see Chap. 5, Reforming Taxes and Customs, for details. All individual tax rates were reduced, and all the remaining taxes were replaced with a flat tax rate system. At the same time, the authorities made it very clear that non-compliance would result in harsh penalties. Specifically, we abolished all exceptions and "special rules" that had previously been granted to members of government, their families, or others who were close to the government in one way or another.

But we didn't stop at reducing the number of different taxes, rates, and fees. Over the course of the next few years, we also revised the wording of ambiguous regulations. For example, there used to be different customs duties for sports shoes (12 percent) and sneakers (0 percent). Similarly, the duty for frozen meat with bones was 12 percent, while there was no customs duty for boneless frozen meat. As a result, Georgia officially never imported any sports shoes or any frozen meat with bones. All imported sports shoes were declared sneakers, and all imported frozen meat, miraculously, turned out to be boneless. To play it safe, importers would routinely bribe customs officers to make sure a given batch of goods was cleared as declared without scrutiny. The regulations were such that both businesses and officials had an incentive to engage in corrupt and illegal practices. The introduction of the new tax code closed most of these loopholes. As a rule of thumb, we tried to make all regulation as clear and precise as possible, and we made sure that all affected parties, public and private, were aware of the applicable laws and rules. To make it even easier for people to contribute to Georgia's growth, we also slashed licenses and permits by nearly 90 percent. We reduced the number of licenses from more than 300 to 41, and the number of permits from over 600 to 53.

2.4   REGULATORY RESTRAINT: LESS IS MORE

At first sight, reducing the number of laws and limiting the role of government may appear counterintuitive as measures in the fight against corruption. But if we look a little closer at human nature, and at the mindset of most bureaucrats in particular, deregulation actually makes a lot of sense as a counter-corruption strategy. Give a government official a desk and a pen, and he will find something to regulate. Occasionally, officials may think that regulation is actually necessary. But more often than not, they will simply come up with new rules to boost their ego, prove that their job is important, or create new opportunities to elicit bribes. This may sound pessimistic, but I have seen it happen in Georgia countless times before 2004, and it is happening in any number of other countries even as you read this. Of course, such self-serving regulation is always marketed to the public as an advancement of the greater good.

Objectively speaking, depending on a country's economic and civic development, different sets of rules and regulations are called for. But in every case, there are two types of rules. On the one hand, there are basic and straightforward rules that are necessary to protect human rights, uphold national security, maintain public safety, safeguard the health of the population, and create a level economic playing field. On the other hand, there is the bulk of byzantine rules that primarily promote corruption and inhibit growth. Adjustments are called for at every stage of a country's development, but the main objective of any government should be to keep non-essential regulation to a minimum. More regulation creates more opportunity for corruption and more obstacles for growth. The more hoops a private company has to jump through to do business, the less likely it is to invest in further growth and create new jobs. Internationally, a moderate regulatory footprint has become a source of strategic advantage among countries competing for foreign investment.

More generally, the size of the government is one of the principal influencing factors of any country's growth. While an outsized government usually slows down economic development, a lean government can speed it up. The size of the government can be measured in two dimensions: financial and regulatory. The government's fiscal footprint is mainly determined by its budget as a percentage of GDP; I will examine this aspect in detail in the next chapter. The government's regulatory heft is less easily quantified, but the number and the level of detail of laws and regulations can serve as proxies. The less developed and the more corrupt a given country is, the fewer rules it should have to make sure it can enforce those rules that are essential to uphold order and promote economic growth. Before 2004, Georgia was clearly on the more unfortunate end of this scale. The country was on the brink of bankruptcy, it was highly corrupt, and it had no culture of following rules. Yet there was an over-abundance of rules and regulations. Most of these were the legacy of Soviet rule or had been introduced around the turn of the millennium, officially to comply with international standards. In theory, this process should have made Georgia a more competitive player in the community of nations. But in reality, almost all of the new rules gave rise to corruption and facilitated personal gain by the ruling elite.

For example, traffic codes in many European countries prescribe that all cars be equipped with a special fire extinguisher. As a rule, it makes perfect sense, and it has doubtlessly saved many lives in developed countries. It was introduced in Georgia in the mid-1990s, but with a twist. Prior to the introduction of the requirement, a high-ranking police official had imported a cheap variety of these special fire extinguishers in bulk. And as soon as the rule became effective, all traffic police officers were instructed to stop vehicles, fine the drivers for not having a fire extinguisher, and tell them where they would be able to buy one. While some drivers actually bought fire extinguishers, most of them just got used to bribing police officers whenever they were caught without one. To make things worse, the equipment was often faulty, but nobody cared once the sale was made or the bribe was paid. After five months, all fire extinguishers had been sold, and from one day to the next, officers stopped harassing drivers about them, as if the risk of fire had suddenly evaporated. Fighting corruption turned out to be much harder than fighting fire.

Another example is the introduction of general inspections for cars in the 1990s. Car owners had to have their vehicle inspected and obtain a document certifying its road worthiness, irrespective of the age of the vehicle. If anything was wrong with the car, the owner was officially obliged to have it repaired. When drivers were stopped by traffic police, they were to show the certificate upon request. The trouble was that the country was so poor that few people could afford the inspection fee, let alone the cost of repairs. At the time, most of the cars on Georgia's roads dated back to the time when the country was still part of the Soviet Union, and almost all of them needed some degree of maintenance. So what happened is that drivers got used to bribing technical inspectors to obtain the certificate, or to bribing traffic police officers if they were stopped without the proper papers. Again, the cause was noble, much as it had been in the case of the fire extinguishers: to increase everyone's safety on Georgia's roads. But it benefited neither drivers nor pedestrians. The only people who benefited were providers of inspection services, usually set up as private companies owned by high-ranking traffic police officials, and traffic patrolmen. The regulation was abolished in 2004. Again, nothing changed, except a decline in bribes paid to the police.

These are just two out of hundreds of similar cases[3] in which regulation was introduced to promote public safety, or some other noble cause, but ended up filling the coffers of corrupt officials, even if this had not been the original intention. Often, such rules were actually triggered by requests from more developed countries in exchange for financial aid. While these previous examples refer to individuals, companies were often subject to similarly questionable rules. For instance, every company would have to endure at least half a dozen inspections annually – by different agencies acting on behalf of the Ministry of Finance, the Ministry of Economy, the Ministry of Agriculture, the Ministry of State Security, and, in some cases, by the prosecutor's office. The only purpose these inspections served was to elicit bribes from the private sector.

Many developing countries today face similar challenges. Foreign governments and international financial institutions press for the introduction of ever more complex rules and regulations, be it to increase their influence in the developing world, or out of sheer ignorance about potential side effects. Sometimes, the justification for new regulation is as trivial as having something to show in return for financial aid. But often, the only effect these new rules have is to engender corruption at the expense of struggling businesses and citizens.

The lesson Georgia learned the hard way is that you cannot impose advanced regulations on a developing country in one fell swoop. In response, the government after 2004 has followed a simple set of guidelines when it came to regulation:

- The country is poor, and the government cannot afford to employ thousands of inspectors to oversee and enforce endless rules and regulations.
- In the past, the government itself and its agencies have been the most corrupt institutions, and at least some officials will likely succumb to corruption again.
- In practice, most rules and regulations are not followed anyway. They do not contribute to the well-being of the population. All they do is cause corruption.
- So let us get rid of all non-essential regulations and simplify the remaining ones to minimize the potential for frustration, confusion, and corruption.
- As the country develops and the economy grows, let us introduce new regulation as it is needed and to the extent that we are able to enforce it.

Following this line of reasoning, Georgia's regulatory framework was reduced to the immediate essentials: fighting corruption, protecting public safety, and collecting taxes. Step by step, we introduced new regulation as it became necessary, and only if we could realistically hope to enforce it. For example, wearing seatbelts in cars became obligatory in Georgia only in 2010. We had considered introducing this rule as early as 2005, but decided against it for two reasons: firstly, because there was no track record of playing by the rules at the time. We would only have created a new source of bribery for traffic police officers. Secondly, and perhaps even more importantly, because we had no way of enforcing such a rule at the time. In 2004, we had laid off the entire traffic police force. In 2005, we were in the process of rebuilding law enforcement from the ground up. And every time you introduce a rule nobody follows, you lose credibility and weaken your stance. But five years later, when people had gradually grown used to paying taxes and respecting the law, the time had come. Now Georgians were ready to accept that regulation was enforced to protect their safety, rather than to elicit illegal revenue streams for government officials. And, finally, we had the kind of police force we could trust to uphold the rules for the sake of public safety, rather than to exploit them for their personal benefit. Almost all drivers immediately started wearing seatbelts when the requirement was finally signed into law in 2010.

As countries mature, governments contemplating the introduction of new regulation should subject prospective new laws and rules to two tests: Do they help maximize growth? And can they be enforced effectively?

2.4.1   *Growth Maximization*

At any given time, a country's regulatory footprint should reflect the stage of its development. This will help promote sustainable long-term growth. Many countries today are overregulated, and in most of these countries a decrease in the regulatory burden will trigger new growth. Think of this interrelation as the regulatory equivalent of the Laffer curve that describes the interdependence of taxation and governmental revenue. An entirely unregulated country will veer toward chaos and, eventually, collapse.[4] There will be no growth whatsoever. A fully regulated country, however, will stagnate, like the Soviet Union did. Sooner or later, the economy will break down unless the government allows for some measure of political change and free enterprise, as the Chinese regime currently does. For every country, there is a point on this regulatory curve that maximizes growth. If there is too little regulation, the country will not be able to realize its full economic potential. If there is too much regulation, this will slow down the economy. While its shape and maximum may vary with political and economic parameters, I believe it is instructive as a concept to help governments practice regulatory restraint (Figs. 2.2 and 2.3).

2.4.2   *Enforceability*

Any regulation that cannot effectively be enforced will result in corruption, or at least in a disruption of political stability and economic growth. Ineffective enforcement will also result in unfair advantages for those who

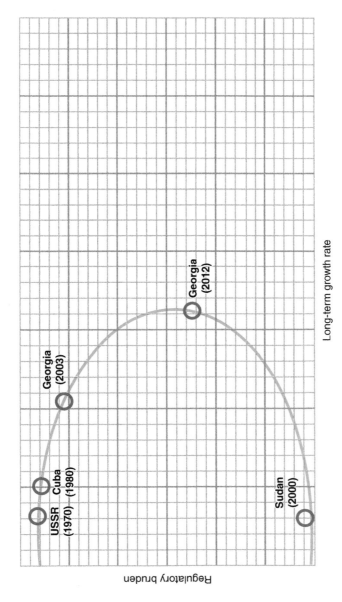

Fig. 2.2 Regulatory curve (conceptual). (*Source*: Nika Gilauri.)

	Permits and licenses
2005	909
2007	137
2012	55

Fig. 2.3 Permits and licenses, 2005–2012. (*Source*: World Bank – "Fighting corruption in public services: chronicling Georgia's reforms.")

elude the rules and disadvantages for those who comply. What is more, a government that introduces rules that it cannot enforce loses credibility. So new rules should only be introduced if the legal system, the government's human resources, and funding enable their enforcement. In the European Union, this is usually not a problem. There is sufficient funding and human capital in the member countries to enforce almost any regulation. This may sound like a good thing but it really isn't since many rules that the European Union creates do not pass the growth maximization test. In contrast, Georgia in 2004 was so underdeveloped, yet so overregulated, that the course of radical deregulation we chose passed both tests. At the time, getting rid of the vast majority of licenses and permits was the right thing to do and quickly brought about economic growth.

In combination, these two criteria – growth maximization and enforceability – will help governments practice regulatory restraint, i.e., introduce new regulation only inasmuch as it promotes stability and prosperity, and if it can be enforced.

2.5   ENFORCEMENT: CHECKS AND BALANCES

Making rules is easy. Making sure people play by the rules is hard. To help the new cohort of public servants stay clean, we set up a strict system of supervision and enforcement. For example, we created a special compliance department in the traffic police force, inspired in equal parts by the concept of mystery shopping[5] and by the zero-tolerance policy pioneered by Rudolph Giuliani.[6] Equipped with hidden cameras, plainclothes agents would intentionally break the law under the eyes of a traffic police officer. They had instructions to offer a bribe if they were stopped. If a given law enforcement officer failed to stop the perpetrator, he was fired. If the officer stopped the agent, but accepted the bribe, he went to prison. If he refused the bribe, he was recommended for promotion or given a bonus.

We took a similar approach to increase compliance among customs officers. Protected by special regulations, compliance inspectors set up shell companies to import goods from neighboring countries. During the customs clearing procedure, the compliance inspector would offer a bribe to the customs officer in charge. Those who accepted the bribe went to prison, those who declined the bribe went free, and those who called for backup to arrest the putative fraudster were promoted.

Additionally, we set up a system of bonuses to reward both those who resisted corruption and those who actively fought it. For lower and middle-level government employees, the rewards were focused on getting them to refuse bribes. For more senior officials, the focus was on new and effective ideas for checks and balances, such as the mystery shopping approach or the introduction of electronic tracking and tracing technology for specific goods such as alcohol and tobacco; see Chap. 5, Reforming Taxes and Customs, for details. Some of the bonuses were as high as three to six times a given official's monthly salary.

Sometimes, however, you have to get even more creative. Take the energy sector. In 2003, Georgia's energy sector was riddled with corruption, but it was almost impossible to convict the culprits. Managers of energy distribution companies simply wrote off theft of energy through illegal lines, or embezzlement of funds, as "commercial losses." To make things worse, energy sector managers were in the habit of sharing their black market gains with government officials to buy their silence. To put an end to this and make sure the energy provided was actually paid for, we declared the collection rate[7] the sector's sole performance indicator. Additionally, we broke the country's biggest distribution company, UDC, down into regional clusters. The grid was split between these clusters in a way that made it very difficult to cheat about the amount of energy received by each cluster. We put a former UDC middle manager in charge of each of the clusters. We reviewed regional collection rates on a monthly basis, and every month, the ten top-performing clusters received a sizeable bonus. We deliberately made the collection rate, i.e., the energy that was paid for as a percentage of the energy that was actually consumed by a given cluster, the only performance metric for these managers to make the bonus system as simple and as transparent as possible. In contrast, the management of the worst-performing clusters was laid off – every month. When we were done, Georgia's energy sector was pretty much corruption-free. The collection rate (including commercial losses) went from 30 percent in 2004 to 91 percent in 2007, one of the fastest improvements of its kind globally.

A similar incentive system was implemented as part of our reform of the higher education sector, another part of the administration that was riddled with corruption. Previously, schools had received funding directly from the Ministry of Education. Schools would routinely bribe government officials to receive extra funds. The principal idea of our reform was to let the money follow students rather than schools. As a first step, we started distributing education vouchers to individuals that replaced direct subsidies to schools. Students and their parents could now freely choose a school – public as well as private, and without any geographical limitation. Schools could convert the vouchers they received from students to cash. This created healthy competition between schools and led to a surge in private school development. As a second step, we extended the concept of motivational performance rewards from institutions to individuals. But instead of introducing a complex scoring system for teachers, principals, and facilities at different types of schools, every high school was simply assessed based on the achievements of its students in university entrance exams, or based on schools' final exams in later years. We chose this metric both because of its simplicity and because it reflected the main interest of students and their parents. The results were widely advertised, thereby intensifying competition between schools for students and their vouchers. For details, see Chap. 10, Education – School Financing and University Reform.

Across the board, we put an end to the exceptions and benefits that had previously been granted to members of the elite. Before, students were only admitted to sought-after university programs if a "protector" made a phone call to university officials, or if they paid a bribe. Students without connections were left out, even if they were smart and worked hard. We were determined not to let this happen again. If there is a rule, it is imperative that it applies to everyone without exception. I firmly believe that this is the only way to establish respect for the rules and make people understand that rules are enforced for their protection, rather than for the sake of oppression or as a source of illegal income for the chosen few. How can anyone expect people to respect the law if even the representatives of the state itself don't respect it, or only if and when it suits them?

2.6 PROCUREMENT – BALANCING TRANSPARENCY WITH FLEXIBILITY

Rules for state procurement are all about finding the golden middle ground. All state procurement is prone to corruption, not only in developing countries. Hence the most important objective for regulation governing procurement is to make the process as transparent as possible and minimize the risk of corrupt deals. At the same time, overly strict procurement rules will limit the efficiency of the government and might make it impossible to acquire the best product on the market. For example, if the rules say that the government must always choose the cheapest option, high-end products will automatically be excluded from the process. Also, there should be different rules for different areas of procurement. Professional services, for example, cannot and should not be procured based on prices alone. Think of marketing, consulting, architecture, and other such intellectual property. Assume a country wants to advertise its investment opportunities in a certain industry, or promote itself as a travel destination on international television. Further assume that the cheapest bidder for the advertising campaign is a local TV station covering one city and half a dozen villages. Chances are that their offer, although it has the lowest price tag, is not the best deal. The most important prerequisite of sound procurement is a solid description of the goods and services to be procured. It should neither be too broad, nor should it be too specific in identifying a particular product if there is a possibility of competition.

In Georgia, the best results in procurement were based on three success factors:

1. *Electronic auction.* The tender and the specifications are put online. Candidates register and bid online. This approach helps the government eradicate ambiguity and rumors. For example, one participant will often tell others that their company already has a pre-arranged deal with the government, and that the others need not even apply. If everything happens online, the process is both transparent and

anonymous. The conditions are clear, but nobody knows who the other bidders even are.

2. *Two-envelope approach*. For every tender, each bidder needs to submit two envelops, one containing the technical description and the other the financial proposal. If the technical description does not meet the requirements, the bidder is excluded from the tender and the second envelop is not even opened. Many governments have adopted this approach, and it generally serves them well. As a next step, the government has two choices: either announce that everybody who passes the quality check has the same chance to win the tender, and that the contract will go to the bidder who offers the lowest price. Or announce that every bidder passing the quality check will be assigned a score for the technical description and that a combined technical-financial score will be generated before the final decision is made.

3. *Two-round price auction*. The government found that companies generally offer better prices in live auctions, where they have a chance to improve their offers, than in sealed envelope auctions. The government decided to combine the merits of both practices and implemented two-round price auctions: Bidders submit sealed envelopes in a first round, then enter a live online auction in which all bidders can improve their prices. Once the technical descriptions are evaluated and finalists are identified, the price envelopes are opened and the prices are disclosed. The bidder with the best price in the envelope is allowed to go last in the online auction. The other bidders follow in ascending order of their initial offers. Every bidder has a three-minute interval to bid, and the best price wins after three rounds of bidding. This approach brought substantial savings in Georgia, and it can easily be adopted by other countries.

2.7   TRUST REGAINED AND BOOKS REBALANCED

As early as 2007, independent observers acknowledged that the post-revolution government had "done better than any [of its] predecessors at battling corruption, standing up to Moscow and respecting civil liberties."[8] In 2010 and 2011, I traveled widely across former Soviet territories and eastern European countries. Georgia was a big topic and, in fact, considered a role model almost everywhere I went. People would ask, if Georgia can end corruption, why can't we? If their traffic police doesn't take bribes, why does ours? If their administration is fast and clean, why isn't ours? Georgian reforms inspired many governments to follow suit. Over the course of the last few years, Georgia has received government delegations from dozens of countries seeking to study and replicate the reforms.

The World Bank itself has published a book-length report[9] that describes the Georgian reforms and promotes the principles on which they are based on globally (see following text for details).

In 2012, it was safe to say that we had won the fight against corruption. In Transparency International's *Corruption Perception Index*, Georgia leaped from the bottom of the table (rank 127 out of 133, below Venezuela) in 2003 to rank 51 in 2012, ahead of Italy.[10] By another measure, Georgia is one of the least corrupt countries in the world. According to the survey-based 2013 *Global Corruption Barometer*, only 4 percent of respondents in Georgia said they had paid any bribes in the past year to any of the eight services that were part of the report, namely police, judiciary, registry, land, medical, education, tax, and utilities. This puts Georgia in the best bracket, ahead of the United Kingdom, where 5 percent of respondents admit to having paid bribes[11] (Fig. 2.4).

At the same time, the Organisation for Economic Co-operation and Development (OECD) acknowledged that "Georgia has achieved significant progress in reducing corruption."[12]

The World Bank's 2012 publication "Fighting Corruption in Public Services – Chronicling Georgia's Reforms"[13] highlights the following success factors:

- Exercise strong political will
- Establish credibility early
- Launch a frontal assault
- Attract new staff
- Limit the role of the state
- Adopt unconventional methods
- Develop a unity of purpose and coordinate closely
- Tailor international experience to local conditions
- Harness technology
- Use communications strategically

% of people that had come into contact with each of institutions listed, that had paid a bribe in the past 12 months

	Education system %	Judiciary %	Medical services %	Police %	Registry and permit services %	Utilities %	Tax revenue %	Land services %	Customs %
GLOBAL	11.0	22.6	12.1	29.0	17.3	9.7	9.5	19.8	22.7
Canada	2.6	3.6	2.2	2.8	3.2	1.4	2.0	4.9	1.6
Denmark	0.1	0.6	0.3	0.0	0.3	0.2	0.3	0.3	0.0
Finland	1.7	0.8	1.0	0.5	0.5	0.8	0.9	0.9	1.4
Georgia	0.9	5.3	2.9	3.2	0.8	1.3	0.0	0.0	0.0
Germany	1.2	0.7	0.7	1.6	1.9	0.9	0.2	0.8	1.1
Israel	2.0	2.2	4.0	1.4	2.0	3.0	1.3	3.4	1.2
Netherlands	2.0	0.0	1.4	2.3	3.2	1.1	1.4	0.0	0.4
New Zealand	2.1	1.7	2.1	3.3	2.8	2.9	1.7	2.5	2.1
Norway	0.5	1.1	0.4	0.4	0.8	0.8	1.2	1.6	1.4
Slovenia	2.0	4.0	3.3	2.4	1.9	1.3	1.0	2.3	4.3
Switzerland	0.3	2.0	0.4	2.1	0.8	1.1	0.4	0.7	4.0
UK	1.4	3.3	0.6	0.9	3.6	0.9	1.2	4.3	4.5

Fig. 2.4 Georgia's performance in Global Corruption Barometer survey ½. (*Source:* TI, 2010/11 Global Corruption Barometer Survey)

2.8 Bonus Systems

Various systems exist to reward civil servants for good performance, e.g., based on key performance indicators (KPIs). Georgia introduced such a system between 2010 and 2012 for the top officials in each ministry, recognizing that their decisions had far-reaching implications for the stability and the prosperity of the country. The KPIs had to be easy to measure. They were negotiated between the relevant minister and the prime minister in front of the rest of the cabinet before the start of each year. For example, foreign direct investment (FDI) and privatization proceeds were the KPIs for the minister of economy. For the tourism department within the Ministry of Economy, the number of tourists served as a KPI. For the minister of energy, the KPIs included net electricity exports and total FDI in the energy sector. In contrast, the minister of healthcare was assessed based on a set of much more diverse, highly specific KPIs, such as the number of newly built hospitals and the decrease in infant mortality. The examples are from 2011, and they reflect the government's political priorities at the time, namely the focus on FDI as the most important driver of Georgia's economy. For some ministries, such as the Ministry of Foreign Affairs, no straightforward KPI presented itself. How do you measure the performance of the minister of the exterior? By counting the number of embassies established, or by the number of motions tabled at the United Nations in a given year? In such cases, we used an average of the KPIs of other ministries. The prime minster reviewed a minister's performance on a quarterly basis. Based on this review, the minister was paid, or not paid, a bonus and given additional funds to reward those among his staff who contributed the most to the good performance of the ministry. In my experience, KPI-based variable pay is a much better way to reward performance than a plain increase in salaries for government employees. It is less of a burden on the budget, it is less politically controversial, and it ties a civil servant's pay directly to the government's agenda.

A more innovative approach to reward the performance of high-ranking civil servants, prevent the misuse of power, promote democracy, and create a better environment for the private sector can be Country Performance Formula (CPF). It is modeled on the practice of publicly traded companies to compensate management (partially) with share options. Typically, only some of these share options can be cashed by an executive immediately. The bulk of such a package is usually subject to a barring clause and can only be cashed in after one, two, or three years. This is to make sure that managers keep the future viability, profitability, and growth of the company in mind. The beauty of the CPF is that it is based on the assessment by an external authority, the stock market, rather than by some internal function or special department.

CPF applies this proven model to the public sector. In my view, 10-year Eurobonds, or comparable debentures, are the best vehicles to play the part of share options for top civil servants:

- The price of Eurobonds is not determined by some department of statistics or the International Monetary Fund, but by financial markets.
- The price is a single figure that reflects all relevant variables, such as the economic development, the political situation, and geopolitical challenges. Also, the price reflects current performance as well as the valuation of future opportunities and risks. For example, the price of the Eurobond will decrease if a country's economic performance deteriorates, or if elections are not free and democratic. It will also go down if unemployment or inflation soars. In contrast, the price will go up if the economic situation, political stability, or international relations improve.
- The price affects public finances and private players alike. If the price goes up, both the state and private enterprises have access to cheaper capital. The whole economy benefits from the lower interest rates that ensue: the state budget, local banks, local companies, and individual borrowers. Also, a higher Eurobond price results in higher-priced local assets, higher prices of local companies, higher income for local entrepreneurs, better visibility of the country on international financial markets, and, hence, more opportunities to attract investors, create jobs, and reduce unemployment.

This is why I believe that the Eurobond is the best basis for the measurement of governmental performance, and that government employees should be rewarded in line with the development of the price of the bond. The formula should be drawn up in such way that a top-performing bond puts civil servants on an even keel with their peers in the private sector in terms of their income.

There is one issue though. Public figures have a tendency to try to hold on to power, sometimes longer than is in the interest of the country, or even, in the worst case, against the will of the electorate. To counter this tendency, the CPF should be set up in a way that puts Eurobond options on hold until government employees have completed their full term without charges of fraud or improper conduct. The term should correspond to a given country's electoral cycles, but not exceed ten years. Some critics argue that the price of Eurobonds may vary with factors that are out of the government's control, such as the global economic situations or geopolitical landslides. This is why the bonus should be based not on the face value of a country's Eurobond itself, but on its performance relative to some reference paper, such as U.S. treasury bonds, or relative to the average of a set of similar countries, or on Credit Default Swaps.

If such a scheme is implemented, the objective of the government will change automatically. The main concern of most members of government is to be re-elected as a party, as a president, or as a cabinet. And governments are often prepared to sacrifice the long-term economic prosperity of the country to short-term populism that will get them re-elected. With a CPF in place, governments will shift their focus to long-term sustainability. If their own income depends on the performance of their country as valued by international financial markets, top civil servants will think twice before committing to higher pensions, or higher welfare payments, without securing the necessary budgetary means.

That said, power itself is still a powerful potion. Some people will try to stay in power regardless of the cost. The CPF will not change the minds of such power junkies. All I am arguing is that a bonus that is based on a country's performance creates an incentive for the average civil servant to balance short-term benefits with long-term prospects. Additionally, the Western world may want to adopt a "Global Magnitsky List" for all corrupt officials; Sergei Magnitsky was a Russian lawyer who uncovered corrupt schemes of the Russian government and was jailed by Russian authorities. He died in prison under suspicious circumstances. Later, the United States Congress adopted a bill according to which all members of the authorities who were involved in the case were deprived of U.S. visas, and their accounts and assets in the United States were frozen.[14] Combining a CPF with such a black list would create a carrot and stick scheme for high-ranking government officials and may help transform the state of developing world within a decade or two.

Ideally, a CPF should be introduced by a government that itself does not benefit from it. In other words, the next government should be the first beneficiary of the formula. This will help resolve concerns about self-enrichment and make it much easier to justify such a scheme in the public eye.[15]

2.9   OUTLOOK

While the impact of deregulation in Georgia was almost universally beneficial, it can also backfire on occasion. For example, there was an institute in Georgia that oversaw the certification of sailors. The institute trained aspiring sailors and awarded them a certificate upon successful completion of the course. These certificates are required for sailors seeking jobs with international shipping companies. But much like the technical inspection service for cars and similar organizations in Georgia at the time, the seaman's institute gave out certificates in exchange for bribes without actually providing any training. In effect, even certified Georgian sailors frequently found themselves insufficiently prepared to work abroad. In response, the government closed down the institute and allowed private companies to offer training and certification for sailors. But it turned out that EU regulation required the certifying body to be a licensed government institute, rather than a private company. As a result, hundreds of Georgian sailors found themselves barred from working on ships that entered EU ports and lost their jobs.

But mishaps like this don't change the fact that regulatory restraint generally helps curtail corruption and promote growth. Fewer and less complex rules provide less opportunity for corrupt officials to elicit bribes or to make life difficult for companies and citizens in other ways. At the same time, restrained regulation also increases the prospects of compliance by the general public. If playing by the rules is comparatively cheap and easy, why would people bother to cheat?

Of course, deregulation must not compromise high-ranking constitutional objectives such as national security, public safety, health, free enterprise, freedom of opinion, and equal opportunity to participate in the pursuit of prosperity. At every stage of a country's economic development and institutional maturity, the government needs to re-assess the adequacy of its regulation and its capability for effective enforcement of the rules. New rules will become necessary, and old rules will become obsolete.

In what follows, I will turn to reforms in specific fields such as taxes, customs, energy, welfare, healthcare, and education. While these areas were faced with different challenges, the fight against corruption permeates almost every aspect of post-revolution reform in Georgia, especially as regards the size of government. Most countries today are overregulated, and the regulatory burden impairs their economic development. But big governments not only slow down growth, they are also more susceptible to corruption. What is true for regulation is also true for government as a whole: Less is more.

NOTES

1. *Roses and Reality in Georgia*, New York Times, November 10, 2007, http://www.nytimes.com/2007/11/10/opinion/10sat3.html (retrieved in 2015). (New York Times 2007).
2. When I started to work for the Ministry of Energy in 2004, my monthly salary was GEL 120, at about two Georgian laris to the dollar, i.e., about USD 60. A head of a department made about GEL 60–80, or USD 30–40, per month. The average salary at the time was about GEL 40, or USD 20.
3. More examples are available if needed, related to International Financial Institutions and/or EU requests.
4. One example of this is Sudan. According to the BBC, South Sudan (split off from Sudan in 2011) in particular has what many describe as a "war economy." See http://www.bbc.com/news/world-africa-34075573 (retrieved in August 2015).
5. Mystery shopping as a concept originates in retail. Manufacturers of consumer goods send anonymous representatives to the stores where the goods are sold. The purpose of these visits is to check whether the goods are stocked, displayed, and priced as agreed between the manufacturer and the retailer. Some companies, such as consumer banks or telecommunications providers, also send mystery shoppers to their own branches to check on sales staff, making sure they follow corporate protocol and provide adequate advice to customers. For details, see Willie Osterweil, *The Secret Shopper*, The New Enquiry, June 4, 2012. (Osterweil 2012).
6. See Norimitsu Onishi, *Be Polite or Else, Giuliani Warns in Announcing Civility Campaign*, New York Times, February 26, 1998 (Onishi 1998).
7. Energy paid for as a percentage of the total energy supplied (not billed).
8. *Roses and Reality in Georgia*, New York Times, November 10, 2007, http://www.nytimes.com/2007/11/10/opinion/10sat3.html (retrieved in 2015) (New York Times 2007).
9. http://documents.worldbank.org/curated/en/2012/01/15647088/ fighting-corruption-public-services-chronicling-georgias-reforms (retrieved in August 2015).
10. http://www.transparency.org/research/cpi/overview (retrieved in August 2015).

11. http://www.transparency.org/gcb2013/results (retrieved in August 2015).
12. http://www.oecd.org/corruption/acn/GEORGIAThirdRound MonitoringReportENG.pdf (retrieved in August 2015).
13. http://documents.worldbank.org/curated/en/2012/01/15647088/ fighting-corruption-public-services-chronicling-georgias-reforms (retrieved in August 2015).
14. Max Seddon and Neil Buckley, *Russia: Magnitsky's bitter legacy*, Financial Times, June 12, 2016 (Seddon and Buckley 2016).
15. A system that is similar to CPF is in place in Singapore. It is, however, not based on the prices of state bonds, but on the average salaries of private-sector CEOs at companies operating in the industry that falls in a given minister's or civil servant's remit. This approach is based on idea that the private sector is the main driver of the economy and that the public sector should do anything to create a better environment for the private sector.

CHAPTER 3

Rightsizing Fiscal and Monetary Policies

Abstract This chapter discusses the right size of government in fiscal terms – identifying characteristics of Budget Optimum – i.e., the parameters of fiscal policy that should contribute to the fast and sustainable economic growth for the particular country in a particular time period. In the first part of the chapter it is argued that budget deficit is not the main parameter of Budget Optimum, but budget to GDP ratio and public expenditure to budget should be examined much closer in parallel with budget deficit. In its second part, this chapter chronicles Georgia's economic recovery plan and its impact on key indicators – making the case for anti-austerity. The third part of this chapter lays out the broader institutional implications of the Georgian reform experience and, suggesting that some rules are outdated, offers innovative concepts – from the management of international financial institutions to cooperation between central banks and governments.

Keywords Budget · Fiscal · Expenditure · Crisis · Formula

Governments can influence a country's economy in two respects: at a financial and at a regulatory level. And I believe that for every country, and at each stage of its development, there is a right size of government in both of these respects. While lessons learned in one country should not blindly be transferred to another, I am convinced that countries at similar levels of

© The Author(s) 2017   43
N. Gilauri, *Practical Economics*,
DOI 10.1007/978-3-319-45769-7_3

development can and should learn from their peers. In the previous chapter, I discussed the economic benefits of controlled deregulation. In the first part of this chapter (Sect. 3.1), I will examine the right size of the government in its fiscal aspect offering a new concept of Budget Optimum – the main characteristics of the budget (and not only budget deficit) that can ensure best economic outcome for that particular moment of that particular economy. In the second part of this chapter (Sect. 3.2), I will make the case of how focusing on the parameters of the Budget Optimum (and not following austerity measures, as advised by many) helped Georgia to recover from the 2008/2009 recession and how this approach may be useful for many countries currently facing austerity measures. In the third part of this chapter (Sect. 3.3), I will examine some of the institutional implications of the experience in Georgia that may be helpful for many developing as well as developed countries in shaping their fiscal and monetary policies during the new economic realities.

I believe there is a Budget Optimum for any economy and it differs based on its level of development and its position in economic cycle. The parameters of Budget Optimum do not take in consideration many budgetary aspects and do not depend only on budget deficit as a main parameter and main measurement of a healthy fiscal policy, but depend on (1) budget to GDP ratio, (2) public expenditure to budget ratio, and lastly (3) the budget deficit as well. I believe that for any economy Budget Optimum can be identified, which will ensure, ceteris paribus, that economy's fastest and most sustainable growth.

3.1   RIGHTSIZING THE GOVERNMENT – BUDGET OPTIMUM

The Georgian case is practical proof that economist Albert Laffer's theory about the relation between taxation and government revenues is right - The bell-shaped "Laffer curve is a representation of the relationship between rates of taxation and the resulting levels of government revenue. [...] One implication of the Laffer Curve is that increasing tax rates beyond a certain point will be counterproductive for raising further tax revenue,"[1] i.e., there is a specific level of taxation that maximizes tax revenue. Others argue that the curve may not be bell-shaped and that it might even have multiple peaks.[2]

In the 2000s Georgia saw two major tax reforms: one in 2004 and one in 2009. As part of the first reform, the number of taxes was reduced and the rates of the remaining taxes were lowered. Most observers predicted a decline in tax revenue but the opposite happened. Tax revenue went up, both in nominal terms and as a percentage of GDP. In nominal terms, tax revenue went from GEL 0.6 billion in 2003 to GEL 6.3 billion in 2013. Of course, GDP growth and inflation contributed to this development. But the relative development of tax revenue confirms that the reforms were successful. Tax revenue as a percentage of GDP went from 7 percent in 2003 to 24 percent in 2012. The impact was already apparent within one year of the first round of reforms.

The reasons for this success are two-fold: improved administration,[3] namely: the fight against corruption in the revenue service department as discussed in the previous chapter; and a realistic tax burden that reflected Georgia's level of development at the time. Before the reforms, the burden was simply too high. Any company attempting to pay the full amount of their tax liability would either have gone bankrupt right away or dug their own grave by increasing prices to an extent that would eventually have driven customers away. Note that Georgia's GDP per capita only came to about USD 922 at the time (World Bank, 2003). So, paradoxical as it sounds, the reduction of the tax level triggered higher tax revenue in Georgia, indicating that the country's pre-reform tax burden was too far towards the right (or the top, depending on the orientation of the graph) on the Laffer curve (Fig. 3.1).

But how can a government determine the appropriate level of governmental revenue as a percentage of GDP? Conceptually speaking, the suitable tax level for any country is that which minimizes corruption and maximizes long-term economic growth without compromising social or political stability. In Georgia, a new tax code was introduced in 2004. Only 6 out of 21 types of taxes remained: two consumption-based taxes, three income-based taxes, and one property-based tax:

1. Consumption-based: Value-added tax (VAT; 18 percent) and customs clearance tax (0/5/15 percent; more than 80 percent of imported goods were cleared at a customs rate of 0 percent)
2. Income-based: Corporate income tax (profit tax; 20 percent, later decreased to 15 percent), dividend tax (5 percent), and personal income tax (25 percent, later decreased to 20 percent)
3. Property-based: Property tax (land tax; up to 1 percent of the value).

On top of these taxes, duties (levies) were introduced for as few as four types of products: tobacco, gas, alcohol, and scrap metal exports. All of

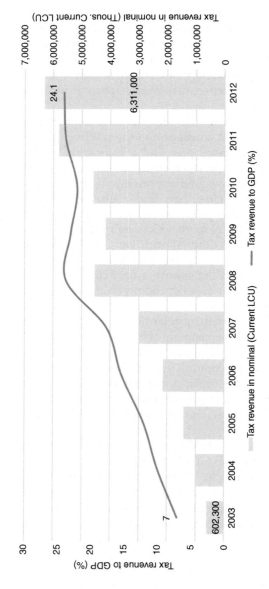

Fig. 3.1 Tax revenue to GDP/tax revenue in nominal. (current LCU) (*Source:* World Bank Group.)

these taxes were flat to incentivize compliance. Any progressive system ("the more you earn, the more you pay") eventually gives rise to corruption; both private individuals and companies will get creative to move into lower tax brackets than warranted by their actual income. What is more, a progressive rate punishes success and, hence, discourages citizens from earning more money and companies from generating higher profits. But in a poor country, you need every incentive that rewards productivity and discourages corruption.

The simple, flat-rate tax system helped Georgia streamline its tax administration and fight corrupt practices in the revenue service department. Also, simplification of the tax system facilitated increase in the degree of compliance and enabled the creation of a relatively level playing field for the private sector. The combined impact of a lower tax burden, a simpler tax code, the successful fight against corruption, and the creation of a level playing field soon led to higher rates of profit and reinvestment. As a result, Georgia attracted foreign investment, GDP rose, and new, higher-paying jobs were created (Fig. 3.2).

Budget to GDP ratio may be the most important aspect of Budget Optimum. When identifying the most optimal Budget to GDP ratio, the factors to be taken into consideration include a country's stage of economic development, level of corruption, volume of international trade, and GDP composition. Database research spanning two and a half decades, since 1980, shows that none of the 18 countries (mentioned in the first chapter) that at any stage of this period had a fast economic growing decade[4] has had a general government revenue (Percent of GDP)[5] to GDP ratio of more than 40 percent; Belarus is the only exception from this rule. Majority of the countries, including Georgia, have had a budget to GDP ratio of below 30 percent, and 5 countries had this ratio between 30 and 40 percent. On the flipside, none of the 23 countries that had a ten-year average general government revenue to GDP ratio of more than 40 percent got anywhere close to doubling GDP per capita in terms of purchasing power parity, or to quadrupling nominal GDP per capita in any ten-year period. These observations might partly be explained by the fact that many of the big spenders are developed countries. The high social obligations that come with their advanced stage of development make it hard for them to keep the budget below 40 percent of GDP, and the maturity of their economies makes it hard for them to achieve fast growth. In any case, a developing country that aspires to catch up with the developed world cannot afford to place a high tax burden on the economy.

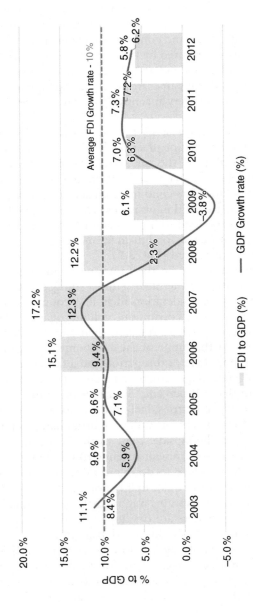

Fig. 3.2 FDI to GDP and GDP growth rate. (*Source*: Ministry of Finance of Georgia.)

3.1.1   Forward-Looking Fiscal Policy

One way of gradually decreasing the tax burden as a percentage of GDP is to increase government expenditure at a rate that is slower than GDP growth. But there is another way of achieving the same objective, and I believe it is more effective in terms of building confidence among market participants and fostering economic growth, an approach I call forward-looking fiscal policy. This requires the government to define and publish a formula according to which the tax burden will be decreased by x percent for every percent of GDP growth for a specified number of years. In other words, all market participants are incentivized to contribute to overall economic growth and are rewarded accordingly. The reduction can be applied, for example, to income tax, corporation tax, or value-added tax.

In some cases, e.g., in an economic crisis, it may be necessary to introduce sectorial taxes, i.e., taxes that only apply to certain industry sectors. In such a situation, I recommend applying the forward-looking approach to the banking sector: decrease the bank tax by x percent for every percent increase in GDP. Why the banking sector? Because banks are enablers of economic growth. Increasing lending and financing activity creates benefits for the economy as a whole. This kind of formula motivates the right people to do the right things, aligning all stakeholders to contribute to increased economic activity. Not only does it help bring down the budget, it also sends a strong signal to the private sector. The formula has not been tested in Georgia, and I am not aware of any country in which it has. Yet I am confident that the forward-looking approach could promote faster recovery from a crisis. Skeptics typically object that banks will always finance sufficiently attractive projects, so why introduce an additional incentive? But forward-looking fiscal policy is not about any particular project. It is about an overall boost to confidence when confidence is needed most. I will explore the economic relevance of psychology and perception in a crisis in more detail in the argument against austerity presented later in the chapter.

3.1.2   One Budget Principle

Another important aspect for rightsizing the government, ensuring the most efficient fiscal policy and thus contributing to Budget Optimum is One Budget Principle, which was adopted by the Georgian government in 2004. In most countries, big parts of government income are earmarked, i.e., reserved for specific types of expenditure. For example, road taxes and levies are often collected based on usage. In France, fees are collected at dedicated toll stations. In Germany, taxes are collected by oil companies through gas stations as a percentage of the price per liter of gas sold. In turn, most countries dedicate taxes collected from road users to the construction of new roads and to the maintenance of the existing network. In Georgia, we opted out of such earmarking of income from specific sources for expenditure in specific areas. All public revenue go into one budget, and all expenditure is financed irrespective of the source of the revenue. The "one budget" principle protects citizens from taxes and levies imposed by competing arms of government, and it increases the agility of government when it comes to public spending.

Take the hotel levy, a duty that is common in many countries. Typically, it goes directly to the ministry or department of tourism, and it is spent to finance advertising campaigns or improve tourism infrastructure. Taken at face value, this allocation appears logical, and it makes it easier to justify a given tax to the public: Tourists should pay for tourism infrastructure, and road users should pay for the road network. But in reality, such levies are rarely sufficient to finance the respective expenditure in full. What is more, roads do not only benefit car owners, but also those who buy and sell any goods that are transported on roads. These effects render the original argument for earmarking practically irrelevant. Moreover, the practice of earmarking has several disadvantages:

- Unhealthy competition among cabinet members and government agencies to create independent sources of income at the expense of the private sector.
- Unnecessarily complex levy systems that give rise to uncertainty and discourage investments – Will there be a new minister who will try to introduce a new levy?
- Inefficient use of government resources – The full cost of administrating a complex levy system can easily exceed the revenues it generates.
- Sub-optimal use of government funds – At any given time, there may be more important, or more urgent, projects than the one a given levy is earmarked for at the time.

In stable times, such inflexibility may merely be seen as inconvenient. But in a crisis, earmarking can become life threatening for the national economy. Imagine the government urgently needs to stabilize the banking sector, but the substantial funds generated from the hotel levy are reserved for staff training in the hospitality sector.

I do not suggest that all levies or excise taxes should necessarily be abolished, although I am convinced that minimizing the number of taxes and surtaxes is good for any economy. Rather, I recommend allocating all government income to one budget. This central budget should be used for the most efficient, or most urgent projects, irrespective of how the income was originally generated. There is one exception to this principle though: those agencies that are in direct contact with citizens, i.e., providers of public services. Such citizen-facing agencies should be allowed to keep part of their income as it creates incentives for them to improve their performance and additional motivation for their staff to provide better service. This will help them evolve from self-serving civil servants into customer-oriented service providers.

Georgia's implementation of the "one budget" principle immediately had the desired effects. Government agencies stopped competing for ever more creative ways to plague the private sector with new duties and levies. Instead, they started competing for the allocation of funds from the budget by developing, proposing, and executing competitive projects. Government became more efficient, more effective, and generally more results-oriented. And as times got tougher, the government had the extra flexibility it needed to take swift and decisive action. Unfortunately, the one budget principle has since been softened. In late 2010, some government agencies were allowed to keep their surplus and spend it on projects identified by the respective ministers, a change that let sectarianism and inefficiency creep back in.

3.1.3 Public Investment Ratio vs. Budget Deficit

Despite the successful reforms, economic growth in Georgia stalled in 2009. This was due to the combined effects of the world financial crisis that had started in 2007 and the Russian invasion of Georgia in 2008. The influx of foreign capital had gone into a sharp decline. The situation was further aggravated by a local political crisis in early 2009. An opposition rally that lasted almost three months had brought economic activity at the center of Georgia's capital, Tbilisi, to a virtual standstill. The economy was heading into sharp recession.

As was expected, recommendations came from every corner to start austerity measures. Typically, austerity has two components:

1. Focus on the budget deficit, i.e., the degree to which public expenditure exceeds public revenue, as the principal indicator of economic health.
2. A policy to maintain or decrease the budget deficit level at all cost, typically by increasing taxes and reducing public spending across the board.

Ever since the worldwide financial crisis, budgetary austerity has been widely recommended to troubled countries globally. Many governments have followed this advice, and most of them have paid dearly. Most recently, Princeton economist and Nobel laureate Paul Krugman has argued that "all of the economic research that allegedly supported the austerity push has been discredited."[6] Yet austerity still features prominently in recovery plans for countries such as Greece, Portugal, Spain, and the Ukraine.[7]

Based on my experience in Georgia, I argue against both components of austerity as defined previously. In particular, I will demonstrate that undifferentiated austerity is not a suitable course of action for a country in a recession.[8] More generally, I believe that the budget deficit as an aggregate figure is insufficient as an indicator of economic health. Specifically, I argue that IFIs put too much emphasis on the deficit as an absolute indicator out of context, when they should rather be looking at its development relative to other economic indicators and more importantly at a public investment ratio (public investment to budget). The Georgian experience shows that a high budget deficit is temporarily acceptable and can even be necessary to allow a country recover from recession, provided a substantial share of the budget consists of public investment. In Georgia, public investment accounted for up to 25 percent of the budget. This allowed the Georgian government to increase the budget deficit to 9.2 percent and then to bring it back down to 3 percent within 2 years. In a recession, public investment can be decreased much more easily politically than other budget positions, e.g., by stretching investment projects over a longer period of time than originally foreseen, or by canceling some projects altogether. What is more, public investment has a much higher multiplier effect on the economy as a whole than other budgetary expenditures, and it contributes to the development of the private sector as well. If external observers and advisers, including the IFIs, assess a country's performance based on the budget deficit alone, they miss out on an important part of the picture. Before putting pressure on a government to reduce the budget deficit, which can have a negative effect on economic development, they should also take into consideration the public investment share in the budget and the effect it has on the economy as a whole.

3.2   Taking a Risk with Anti-austerity

When Georgia was on the brink of a sharp economic slump in the beginning of 2009, our government opted against austerity. Instead of raising taxes and cutting public spending, Georgia chose to take the path of controlled expansionary monetary and fiscal policy. In early 2009, the government and the National Bank of Georgia made a joint statement, announcing a tax reduction, an increase of the budget deficit, decrease in social expenditure but significant surge in public investment and a number of banking regulation measures that would make it easier and cheaper for private companies to borrow money (in parallel policy rate was reduced significantly from 12 percent in Q3 of 2008 to 5 percent in Q4 2009). In many ways, this was the direct opposite of austerity – the measure that many had advised. But we felt we didn't have a choice. With memories of the recent Russian invasion still fresh, all the leading players in Georgia's private sector were even more scared than those in neighboring countries. Both the government and the National Bank were convinced that announcing austerity measures would have driven the country into an even deeper recession, and possibly into eventual bankruptcy. That was my crucible as Minister of Finance. I took a chance by decreasing the income tax rate from 20 percent to 15 percent, instead of increasing taxes. My decision was based on meticulous calculations, but many experts had advised me against it. The reduction took effect in 2009, on January 1. Six weeks later, I was appointed Prime Minister. At the time, Georgia's economy was shrinking at a rate of –8.7 percent. I guess this was why nobody else wanted the job.

Georgia opted against austerity and quickly regained its footing. By the end of 2009, GDP decline was down to –3.9 percent, lower than in any other country in the region, and Georgia was the first among its peers to recover in 2010 with a growth rate of 6.4 percent. What is more, the budget deficit was brought back down to pre-crisis levels within two years' time after the joint declaration of what is now frequently referred to as the Fast Economic Recovery Plan. The debt to GDP ratio, which had temporarily increased to more than 40 percent, was brought back down to 34 percent. When I retired from the position of prime minister in 2012, Georgia's economy (in that quarter) grew at a rate of 8.2 percent. Within three years period a turnaround from −8.7 percent (second quarter of 2009) to +8.2 percent was made (second quarter of 2012) – nothing short of an economic miracle (Fig. 3.3).

3.2.1   What Georgia Did

One of the first and most drastic measures we took was to cut taxes. Starting in 2004, the tax code had already been simplified dramatically. But instead of returning to pre-reform tax rates to balance the budget, as many other governments have chosen to do in similar situations, taxes were further reduced (Fig. 3.4).

Additionally, we allowed the budget deficit to increase – not at random or permanently though, but in a highly targeted fashion and for a limited period of time. The deficit went from 4.8 percent in 2007 to 6.4 percent in 2008 and 9 percent in 2009, albeit for one year only. Within two years of reaching its peak, the deficit was brought back down to 3.6 percent in 2011 and to 2.8 percent in 2012. All additional expenditure was allocated to infrastructure, such as highways and high-voltage power lines – projects that had the potential to generate additional private sector activity. Examples include the construction of a new high-voltage power line connecting the Georgian energy grid to the Turkish energy grid, enabling Georgia to export electricity generated from hydropower to Turkey and attract investments in the construction of new power plants in Georgia. Public investment as a percentage of the total budget went from 20 percent in the late 2000s to 25 percent in 2012. At the same time, social subsidies and the government's payroll bill were reduced. Only these cuts were in line with the austerity measures proposed by many, and they were deemed necessary at the time to free up as much capital as possible for public investment.

Other components of the recovery plan included the privatization of state-owned enterprises and the issuing of Eurobonds on international financial markets to attract more foreign funds and accelerate the modernization of Georgia's economy. For example, state-owned companies, such as

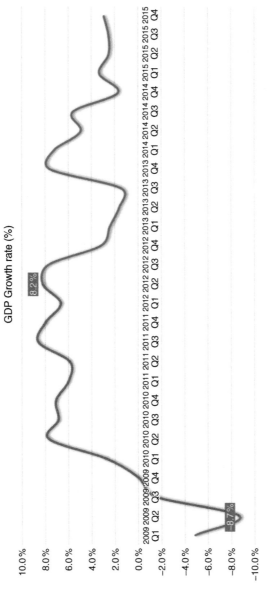

Fig. 3.3 GDP growth rate in Georgia. (*Source:* Georgian National Statistics Office.)

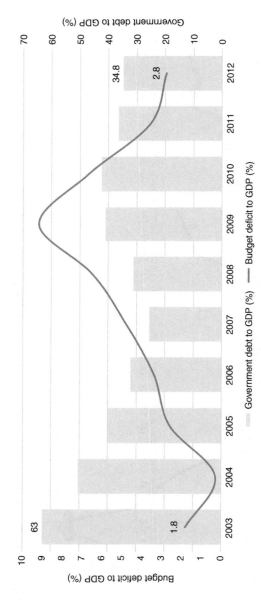

Fig. 3.4 Budget deficit to GDP/government debt to GDP. (*Source*: National Bank of Georgia; Ministry of Finance of Georgia.)

Georgian Railways and the Georgian Oil and Gas Corporation issued Eurobonds at the London Stock Exchange. The proceeds helped us finance additional infrastructure projects and draw more international capital.[9] In parallel, banking sector regulation was loosened to make it easier for Georgian banks to finance recovery at first and then renewed growth.

3.2.2   Why It Worked

The Fast Economic Recovery Plan was a resounding success. Georgia quickly came out of the recession. I believe that this lasting success owes as much to psychology as it owes to economics. In a recession, everybody is scared. Consumers fear unemployment and tax increases. As a result, they stop spending and start saving, reducing the size of the economy almost immediately. Private sector players, fearing instability, will hold off on major investments and postpone new hires, curbing GDP growth and driving up the unemployment rate. Foreign investors fear for their capital and flock to other countries. In other words, fear is the biggest enemy of the national economy in a recession.

While I respect all economic theories, and the sophisticated concepts economists have come up with to explain economic development, I am convinced that the behavior of individuals and markets is best explained by looking at their perceptions. The economy is driven by the perception of its participants, and the most important participant is the private sector. I believe that governments cannot create jobs in the long term or drive economic growth all by themselves. But what governments can do is create an environment in which entrepreneurs have the confidence to invest and create jobs. So the best thing the government can do in a recession is to foster stability, or at least the perception of stability. A recession can have many causes – an ineffective government; inadequate regulation; or external factors, such as geopolitical issues or trade wars. Regardless of what those reasons are, the best thing the government can do is to create a sense of stability and predictability. In a recession, entrepreneurs are especially scared, and they have every right to be scared. They don't know to what extent the economic decline will affect their companies, their personal income, and their lives. They don't know how long the situation will last. They don't know how the government will react. Many theorists will say that this is precisely what being an entrepreneur is all about – dealing with uncertainty and hedging risks. But why create additional uncertainty when the government can contribute to engendering stability?

Consumer confidence is a crucial driver of recovery. But most consumers don't pay much attention to government policy, let alone GDP growth rates. Their perception of the economic situation is shaped by the private sector. Are the revenues of the companies they work for declining? Do they see worried looks on the faces of their bosses and colleagues? Is there talk of downsizing? Are their friends and family members losing their jobs? Are they personally in danger of being let go by their employers? Any of these signs will cause them to stop spending and start saving. The same is true for public servants. If they see budgetary revenue go down and the government start making budget cuts, they will fear for their jobs.

So nerves in the private sector are understandably frayed in a recession. Entrepreneurs need to adjust to a new reality, and their main concern is the lack of predictability. Consumers are apprehensive too. They start saving instead of spending. This triggers a vicious circle of economic decline. If, on top of all this, the government announces austerity measures, even more uncertainty, and ultimately chaos will ensue.

It is my firm belief that the worst thing that any government can do in a recession is to create or increase uncertainty. When some European countries announced austerity measures during the financial crisis, they set off a downward spiral even before the measures were enacted. Fear of tax increases, instability, and unemployment turned into a self-fulfilling prophecy.[10] Examples include Greece, Portugal, Spain, and many other countries.

During a recession, governments should not be forced to decrease their budget deficit by cutting expenditure and increasing taxes. Budget cuts will only aggravate the situation, chiefly because governments will be inclined to decrease public investments rather than social expenditure because social cuts are unpopular with the electorate. Tax increases also have a detrimental effect, since they make it even harder for private enterprises to generate a profit and stay in business without succumbing to illegal practices. Higher taxes also make the economy as a whole less efficient by shifting funds from the more efficient private sector to the less efficient public sector. Instead, governments should decrease social expenditure, and they should be allowed to increase their budget deficits temporarily, even through higher debt, to finance public investment that drive additional private sector activity and reduce taxes. Depending on a country's debt profile, the higher budget deficit could be financed through international financial institutions or financial markets. This will initially increase a country's debt to GDP ratio, but the recovery typically brings it back to a healthy level within few years. Sadly, many countries were forced to decrease budget deficits expecting their debt to GPD ratios to fall in the last financial crisis. This led to a decline in economic activity and negative growth or stagnation. As a result, debt to GDP ratios are not coming down as quickly as they would have with the help of temporary expansionary policies. In many cases, the debt to GDP ratio actually increased because of the decline in economic activity (Fig. 3.5).

In Georgia's case, the decision to keep spending even under duress sent a signal of stability and engendered confidence among all market participants.[11] By decreasing taxes and focusing public expenditure on infrastructure, rather than social subsidies, we sent a clear message: the government is committed to the creation of a stable environment for domestic enterprise, foreign investment, and private consumption. We even loosened banking regulations and monetary policy. We issued Eurobonds to finance more infrastructure projects and compensate for the foreign direct investment that had dried up in the aftermath of the Russian invasion. The perception these measures created were at least as important as their direct economic impact: we have reached the low point. From now on, we are on the way up. Good times are ahead of us, and we will come out of the recession very soon. In record time, this perception became the new reality. The recession lasted only a few months. Businesses started to invest in growth and hire more people. Consumers became more confident and started to spend money again, rather than hoard it. As a result, Georgia averted bankruptcy and came out of the recession within just one year, faster than any other country in a similar situation. The psychological effects of the government's actions helped Georgia overcome its double trouble long before our investments could have taken actual economic effect. Of course structural reforms, cuttign red tape, improving governemnt services, increasing state institutions' efficienies that had already been government's priotiy has also contributed significantly to the fast recovery.

In other countries facing similar challenges, talk of austerity measures created a growing fear of budget cuts, higher taxes, less economic predictability, increased unemployment, and declining consumer spending. By announcing austerity measures, governments in those countries set off a vicious cycle of negative perception, often before the measures were even implemented. Had the International Monetary Fund (IMF) and its associates been less concerned with the sheer short-term budget deficit and more mindful of the total structure of the budget (including budget to GDP and public expenditure to GDP – Budget Optimum) and simple structural reforms, the situation would have been very different in many

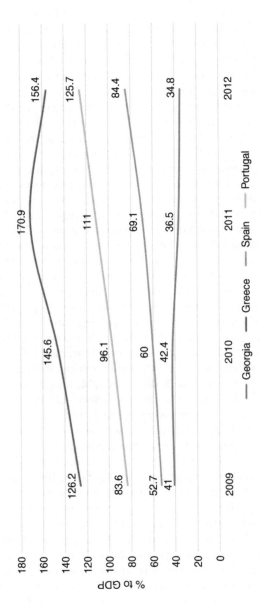

Fig. 3.5 General government gross debt to GDP. (Portugal, Greece, Spain, and Georgia – comparison) (*Source:* IMF, Ministry of Finance of Georgia.)

countries still stagling with economic recovery. Looking ahead, my advice to governments is to exercise prudence and create a financial cushion by keeping the deficit low when the economy is growing.

In a nutshell, here is how Georgia overcame the recession without submitting to blunt austerity as recommended by IFIs:

- Repeated tax and customs simplification and reduction
- Controlled, temporary budget deficit increase despite the crisis and adopting One Busget principle
- Re-allocation of funds from social expenditure to investment in infrastructure
- Focus on the ratio of investment to budget, rather than on budget deficit alone
- Privatization of state-owned enterprises
- Issuing Eurobonds for remaining public assets to raise additional funds
- Deregulation of the private sector and structural reforms
- Special rules for the banking sector to increase its lending capabilities

While governments may not be able to create jobs in the long run, government policy can create an environment in which entrepreneurial activity will flourish and consumers will be sufficiently confident to spend what they make. Whatever the cause of a given recession, the best any government can do is help create a sense of economic stability. When people panic, things start falling apart.

3.3   INSTITUTIONAL IMPLICATIONS

Based on the experience of fighting recession, creating new formulas for economic recovery and growth, and analyzing the fast changing economic environment, few innovative concepts can be shaped in regard to fiscal and monetary policies. Most theoretical economists purport that foreign financial aid is a good thing for a country in distress, that there must be a Chinese Wall between central banks and governments, and that inflation is a bad thing. Practical economists, however, should be prepared to challenge such textbook paradigms in light of the real-life situation in a given country at a given time. Based on my experience in Georgia, I show in what follows that sometimes foreign aid comes with so many strings attached that it is as much a burden as it is a blessing, at least until the government takes control to shape the agenda and coordinate the contributions of foreign donors. Furthermore, I argue that, although the independence of central banks must be preserved, some measure of official cooperation between central banks and governments can be beneficial, and that moderate inflation (higher than most of the Central Banks currently are targeting for) can be a good thing.

3.3.1   IFI Assistance Can Be a Liability

IFIs have fairly deep pockets. If their resources are put to good use, they can make a huge difference for a developing world – improve existing infrastructure, boost private sector activity, and increase the confidence of entrepreneurs and investors. And working with IFIs is not only a source of financing, it also provides an opportunity to learn from international experience. Unfortunately, many governments do not fully understand the mechanisms of IFI financing and fail to utilize it properly. Without proper coordination by the government of the receiving country, IFI projects have a tendency to take on a life of their own. In fact, the bureaucratic burden can outweigh the actual benefit. This is what happened in Georgia in the early 2000s. But when the government took control of the agenda and started pulling the right levers in a coordinated fashion, the productivity of the assistance soared. After the Russian invasion of Georgia and the donor conference held in Brussels in October 2008, IFI assistance was handled with aplomb and efficiency by everyone involved, resident IFI representatives and members of government alike. It was a successful joint effort. Although it took more than half a decade for the aid to take effect, the political and economic support was a major factor in getting the country back on track. But this was years later, and Georgia had to climb a steep learning curve to get there.

3.3.1.1 Lack of Coordination
As soon as the new Georgian government was appointed in 2004, we realized that IFIs had set aside substantial financial resources for Georgia but that these resources were not used efficiently. The reason for the inefficiency was two-fold: IFIs were not sufficiently coordinating their work with the government, and each IFI wanted to participate in as many projects as possible. Unless the government takes charge and defines the agenda, IFIs end up competing with each other, or even with themselves internally, trying to maximize

everything that will make them look active and involved: the number of loans and grants they disburse, the number of areas pre-approved for assistance, and the number of conditions and stipulations imposed on a given loan or grant. Without proper oversight and coordination, this tendency can turn foreign aid into a race that is more about the formal scores and check marks than about the actual outcomes. Even today, many governments are struggling with this issue.

3.3.1.2 Conflicts of Interest

In Georgia, we found that representatives of different IFIs went from door to door at ministries and government agencies, trying to persuade them to take advantage of yet another loan or grant. In many cases, different IFIs offered funding to the same institution to address the same issue, only under different titles. Initially, the members of the new government were more than happy to accept such grants or special loans. But after a few months, we began to understand that there were many strings attached to these apparent acts of charity. In my own experience, grants can do even more harm than loans if they are not managed properly. This is because grants are typically contingent on the introduction of new regulation or changes to existing ones. These regulatory initiatives are driven by an IFI's own policy, rather than by the agenda of the government of the receiving country. Once a given policy has worked in one country, decision makers at IFI headquarters are inclined to prescribe it to every other country. Resident representatives of IFIs, eager to please their higher-ups by promoting the in-house agenda, will push such policies onto the government. In Georgia, this often led to conflicts of interest. IFIs would advocate one thing, but Georgia needed another.

When we brought up the issue, IFIs said that their grants were not part of the government's budget anyway. Their representatives promised they would do the necessary research, pay for the experts, and even draft the required legislation or regulation. At first sight, it's a compelling argument: advanced regulation, based on best practices, is introduced at no cost to the state. But when you take a closer look, this arrangement is not such a good deal. The opportunity cost is substantial:

- The funds allocated to a project driven by an IFI's agenda could be used for another cause that is in line with the agenda of the elected government. But if the government doesn't make a dedicated effort to coordinate and prioritize, IFIs will proceed with their projects based on approval from a particular institution, agency, or official, rather than from the government per se.

- Each additional project takes up a little more of the government's human resources. What is more, high-caliber civil servants often quit their jobs to join the ranks of IFIs, which pay higher salaries than the governments of most developing countries can afford, often for less work. Both effects weaken the government.
- The urge to introduce new regulation puts an additional burden on the government itself. Once their money is spent, IFIs will lobby to have the new regulation signed into law and bring up the issue at any meeting with officials. Resident IFI representatives themselves are often under pressure from their respective headquarters to deliver on a given cause or policy change, regardless of the actual value it creates for a country's economy in a given situation.

That said, governments are at least as much to blame for these problems as the IFIs. It is the responsibility of the government to make sure that IFIs work closely with them and align their efforts with the governmental agenda. If this process of coordination and communication is not sufficiently clear and determined, IFIs will take things into their own hands.

As soon as these hidden costs and side effects were properly understood, the Georgian government started making a big effort, and spent a lot of time and resources, pushing back against regulations that were in conflict with the government's agenda, or not sufficiently aligned with Georgia's stage of development. Sometimes we succeeded, sometimes we didn't. Examples include:

- An IFI had dedicated financial resources to drafting a law that makes third-party insurance obligatory. While such regulation may be relevant and beneficial in other countries, Georgia at the time was not at the stage of development that would have warranted the introduction of obligatory third-party insurance. What is more, we were opposed to any obligatory schemes as a matter of principle.
- Another IFI had drafted regulation regarding deposit insurance. Georgia had never had deposit insurance regulation before, and it was not introduced despite the IFI's continued efforts and

warnings. Nevertheless, thanks to sound banking regulation, Georgia was one of very few countries that did not suffer a single bankruptcy of a bank during the world financial crisis (2007–2009). Almost every other country in the region experienced such bankruptcies, and many of them had trouble protecting or refunding deposits, although they had deposit insurance schemes in place.

- In another case, an IFI spent USD 40 million on what their representatives referred to as business environment support. But none of the members of the Georgian government involved in improving the business environment can recall any contribution from this project. What everybody remembers, however, is that the project absorbed massive financial resources and kept many of Georgia's finest civil servants occupied for almost four years.
- There was also an IFI that proposed a new law that would govern tourism, including a long tail of regulations and guidelines, such as Western-style certification standards for hotels and restaurants. At the time, however, Georgia's tourism infrastructure was not ready for such regulation. All it would have brought is additional obstacles for investors in the hospitality sector, additional expenses for existing businesses, and additional need for government oversight that might well have given rise to a new wave of corruption. We stopped the introduction of this regulation, and the development of the tourism sector has proven us right. Today, tourism is widely regarded as one of Georgia's most dynamic sectors. The number of visitors to Georgia increased from 350,000 in 2004 to 5 million in 2012 – without any complex tourism legislation.

Of course, there were also some examples of effective IFI initiatives in Georgia. Whenever IFI efforts were closely coordinated with the government, and the government was able to implement the respective reforms, the results were very positive. For example, the voucher financing scheme for schools had been suggested by IFIs as early as the year 2000. But the government at the time was unable to conduct the deep reforms that were required for the scheme to succeed. When the new government made education reform one of its top priorities and reversed the flow of financing from schools to students, the scheme was a big success.

3.3.1.3 Issues with Loans

As far as IFI loans are concerned, there are two main issues: competition and fragmentation. As investors, IFIs partly compete with the private sector and local financial institutions, instead of cooperating with them, as they should. What is more, their activity is often all over the place, rather than focused on the areas that are most important to the development of a given country. In Georgia, the IFIs were so eager to utilize the resources they had set aside for the country that they started to compete with and crowd out the private sector, thereby disrupting the market and hindering the development of a free economy. Because they have access to substantial funds at low interest rates, IFIs can afford to cherry-pick the most promising projects, often snatching them from local financial institutions. But the idea is for IFIs to cooperate with the local economy, not to compete with it. Additionally, IFIs strive to build as diverse a portfolio of relatively small loans as possible, sometimes regardless of the real priorities for a given country at a given time. In many cases, multiple IFIs were pushing loans on the government in the same area. And they all wanted to have their own, dedicated project implementation unit and get involved in as many regulatory discussions as possible. From the perspective of resident IFI employees, this behavior is quite understandable: they were simply hedging their bets. By investing in as many projects as possible, they would always be able to report some success to their respective headquarters, even if the majority of projects fell through. This proliferation created a lot of friction, distraction, and inefficiency at a time when what Georgia needed most was focus.

3.3.1.4 The Special Coordination Team

How did we solve the problem? By creating a clear format for cooperation. We set up a special coordination team as the sole gatekeeper for all IFI projects. The team consisted of members of all ministries and agencies receiving IFI grants or loans, as well as of all IFI representatives. It was headed by the minister of finance. In special cases, the prime minister himself got involved. Based on negotiations in the coordination team, specific projects were assigned to specific IFIs, and these IFIs were discouraged from participating in other projects. For example, it was agreed that most of the World Bank's funds would be spent on road infrastructure in East Georgia. JICA, the Japan International Cooperation Agency, was asked to focus on road infrastructure in West Georgia, i.e., the coastal region. ADB, the Asian Development bank, would make the renewal of regional water utilities its priority. EBRD, the European Bank for Reconstruction and Development, would focus on the energy and financial sectors, while KfW, the Kreditanstalt für Wiederaufbau, would help reform and rebuild the energy sector infrastructure. If any of these institutions chose to get active in other areas, it was at their own risk. The government would take no responsibility for such off-agenda initiatives, neither for the projects themselves nor for the loans used to finance them.

Initially, the IFIs were opposed to this approach. They would have preferred a diversified portfolio of projects and regulatory debates so they would always have something to report to headquarters. But eventually, they saw that our clear-cut approach was more effective and more efficient. Because they devoted their full attention to the areas of priority we had assigned them, all the resident IFI representatives soon had major success stories to report. It's simple really: if you are placing one big bet, rather than a large number of small ones, you will do everything to see it succeed. But coordination was only one aspect of how the government took control of IFI aid. Additionally, the relevant minister had to demonstrate to the government, for every proposed grant or loan, that the respective project would benefit the country and would not cause any additional regulatory burden. During the first few months after this rule was put in place, almost 90 percent of all such proposals were rejected. But before long, both the IFIs and the relevant government agencies understood that proposing a project that would not advance the government's agenda was futile.

In fact, the system worked so well that it attracted additional funds to Georgia. After a while, IFIs offered to increase their investment in Georgia in case any of the neighboring countries did not fully utilize their allotted funds. In the end, Georgia received more financing from IFIs than it was pledged during the 2008 donor conference in Brussels.

3.3.1.5 Lessons Learned

The energy sector is, perhaps, the most instructive example of how IFI projects can add value when the government coordinates them. When I became Minister of Energy, I found that IFIs had written up a number of development plans for the energy sector. These plans, however, partly contradicted each other and none of them was applicable to the situation in Georgia. Had Georgia followed one of these plans, it would still be a blacked-out country today. But when we, as the government, sat down with IFI representatives to discuss and determine the real needs of the energy sector in Georgia, the results were outstanding. Examples of successful projects that drove sustainable change in the sector include:

- Renewal of hydroelectric power plants
- Construction of new transmission lines
- Metering program for distribution companies
- Implementation of management contracts

The reform of the energy sector was a major driver of change for the better in Georgia. Examples of similarly successful IFI-backed projects include the construction of highways and local regional roads, water utility renewal, and the injection of capital into Georgia's banking sector to offset the effects of the world financial crisis and the Russian invasion. These were all landmark projects that prepared the ground for private sector development, jumpstarted the economy, and gave confidence to investors. All successful projects had three things in common:

1. Close coordination between IFIs and the government
2. Focus of each IFI on a specific sector or major project
3. Full commitment of the government to these projects

Can our experience in Georgia help shape IFI activities in other developing countries? I believe that it can. IFIs have huge financial resources that can make a big difference in the developing world. I believe that such aid is most effective, and most efficient, when IFIs ask a few fundamental questions before they start spending money. Why not cooperate with a country's elected government instead of pushing a particular agenda? Why not focus on major infrastructure projects that will accelerate private sector development and attract further investments, rather than build a huge portfolio of sub-critical projects? Why not pursue broad objectives, such as GDP growth and a decrease in unemployment, instead of pushing a particular regulatory agenda? Why not hire top consultants for specific studies, rather than try to do everything in-house?[12] Why not support the implementation of new management contracts for state-owned enterprises to fight corruption, introduce a modern management style, nurture new generations of leaders, and import know-how from other countries? And finally, why not take civil servants from developing countries on study tours to other countries to enable them to learn from successful reformers, rather than offer grants to write new regulation? Once civil servants see with their own eyes what a specific reform is all about, they will be in a great position to adapt the underlying principles to their own country. I believe that enabling local officials to turn things around is a much more sustainable form of assistance than writing laws. If you give people a fish, you feed them for a day. As the saying goes: if you teach them how to fish, you feed them for a lifetime. I believe that reflecting on these questions will help IFIs in their efforts to make the world a better place.

3.3.2   No More Chinese Walls?

Time and again, careless governments have allowed inflation to run wild by printing money, especially prior to elections, when economic growth and decreasing interest rates are more important than the fight against inflation. As a direct result of such shortsighted, irresponsible behavior, central banks have gained positions of total independence as guardians of the currency. Ever since Paul Volcker, Chairman of the U.S. Federal Reserve under Jimmy Carter and Ronald Reagan, successfully battled the surging inflation by increasing the policy rate against the expectations of the government in the 1980s,[13] few people have challenged the independence of central banks and their right to oversee monetary policy.

However, economic challenges are changing, and economic policy should evolve in step with these changes. Today, inflation is not the biggest issue anymore in most of the developed world. Instead, many countries are facing a threat of deflation and struggling with a demand-driven deceleration of the economy. While I don't suggest that governments return to a regime of printing money at will, I think it's time to tear down the Chinese walls that have been erected to limit cooperation and let central banks and governments work together in the best interest of their countries. In some cases, the independence of central banks is very useful, especially to prevent dangerously high inflation rates. In other cases, however, close cooperation between a country's central bank and its fiscal authority (typically the ministry of finance) can be much more effective than the independent actions of either entity. May be it is time to break down taboo and consider the following policies:

1. Expand the objectives for central banks from inflation prevention to inflation prevention and economic growth.

2. Establish a council consisting of the heads of fiscal and monetary authorities and maybe even the head of government. Have the council convene regularly to review the development of the national economy.

3. Every two to three years, put in place an agreement between the central bank and the ministry of finance, outlining the key parameters of fiscal and monetary policy.

4. Empower this council to implement all necessary measures needed for the given stage of development of the economy, may it be managing the supply of money through coordinated measures or giving funds directly to the government, provided there is consensus among the members of the council (so-called helicopter money).

Currently, many countries have no mechanism to fund the government's budget directly by printing money, even if all parties agree that this is the right thing to do in a given situation. But why punish future generations for mistakes governments made decades ago?

Critics will say that governments might be tempted to abuse the controlled collaborative approach I propose, especially in developing countries, where checks and balances are not well developed and institutions are relatively weak. That may be the case, and I'm all for precautions that will help avoid such abuse. But what critics don't see is that it is already going on – behind closed doors anyway. Formally, central banks in many developing countries are independent, in line with the rules and regulations that have been established in compliance with the requirements of IFIs or developed countries. But in reality, central banks and governments in many countries are cooperating closely, often, but not always, with the best interest of the national economy in mind. I believe that such off-the-record dealings should cease, and that they should be replaced by clear, transparent rules and regulations for cooperation. I am convinced that all parties would benefit from such an arrangement, including the central banks. Specifically, formalized cooperation would lead to more balanced decisions and shared responsibilities. Today, the heads of central banks often act as lone warriors, even where supervisory boards exist. As a result, decisions that might be perceived as painful or unpopular are frequently delayed or avoided. The joint council that I propose would be better equipped to deal with challenges that affect not only the currency but also the entire economic stance of a country, in a timely and effective fashion.

This was the case in Georgia, and it helped us overcome multiple crises and challenges. Even though there was no legally established council between the government and the National Bank of Georgia, and no contracts had been signed by these institutions, cooperation was very close. In many cases, fiscal and monetary policies were coordinated. This approach was particularly useful during the economic growth period and when the world financial crisis hit Georgia in the aftermath of the Russian invasion (2009 and 2010). Joint efforts by the government and the National Bank of Georgia helped Georgia emerge from the crisis faster, and in better shape, than any other country in the region.

3.3.3   Inflation Can Be an Asset

Even though inflation targeting is the main policy of many central banks, still the targets themselves mostly are not derived from the best possible mix of economic growth and acceptable level of inflation. As it has already been mentioned previously, central banks are charged with a gatekeeper-from-inflation role, and for them keeping inflation as low as possible is the top priority – not taking in consideration the economic growth forgone due to such policies. Let me take the argument against overly rigid inflation control one step further. I believe that moderate inflation can be a good thing – not any kind of inflation, and not in all situations of course. In the twentieth century, inflation has wrecked many economies and inflicted incredible hardship on many people. But I have also seen inflation act as an investment accelerator, and I think governments should take advantage of this phenomenon. While high inflation is bad, deflationary pressure can also have detrimental effects on the economy – less dramatic perhaps, but potentially more prolonged. And if demand-driven economic slowdown and deflationary pressure coincide, even strong economies can suffer and find themselves facing a recession. Examples include Japan, for the past three decades, and the European Union, for almost past decade.

Look at it this way. Assume you want to buy a house. Prices go down, so you decide to wait a while. You want to get a good deal, and what is the harm in holding out for a few weeks? An investor considering to buy another company will behave in much the same way, hoping that the valuation of the target will decrease. Or put yourself in the shoes of a manufacturing company. You need to buy materials, but consumer prices are now lower than they were when you made your profit calculations, and they are still declining. Assume that manufacturing the finished products takes some time. Won't you hesitate to buy those costly materials when you don't know whether you will be able to generate enough revenues to cover your costs and turn a profit in the end? In a deflationary period, economies frequently slow down because of the cumulative effect of such delayed decisions ("investment decision gap").[14] During a period of moderate inflation, this effect is reversed. The house buyer, the investor, and the manufacturer will all seek to move quickly and close their deals when they see prices going up.

The case for an acceptable level of inflation – see following text for what I consider "acceptable" – is even stronger for developing countries. They benefit from nominal GDP growth, if only because of the psychological effect it has on market participants. Of course, inflation does not bring real GDP growth. But let's face it: many international investors look at nominal GDP per capita as their most basic indicator of whether a given country even deserves their attention. Because of such filtering, it can make all the difference for a developing country to which nominal GDP per capita bracket it is allocable: Below USD 1000? 1000 to 5000? 5000 to 10,000? Above 10,000? Many investors will not give a second thought to why exactly a given country suddenly pops up on their GDP radar as a middle-income country, or even a higher middle-income country. Is it due to a slightly higher inflation rate, or because of real economic growth?

An additional benefit of moderate inflation is the fact that it can lift part of the burden of social expenditure. Inflation increases nominal tax revenue. And if a country's formulas for welfare and social support do not account for inflation, social expenditure stays the same, leaving the government with additional funds. The surplus can be used for investments or increases in social assistance, as warranted by the political situation.

So what is an "acceptable" level of inflation? I believe that the acceptable rate is contingent on a country's specific situation and recent economic history. If market participants have had – and still remember – an experience of an inflation rate of x percent hurting their businesses and their livelihoods, then x is too high a rate. Generally, the highest acceptable level of inflation is the rate beyond which savings increase only because of inflation. It is the level beyond which individuals and business grow fearful of hyperinflation and start spending less, consuming less, and saving more. It is the level beyond which market participants lose their faith in a stable future. For Georgia, that rate is somewhere under 9–10 percent. When inflation exceeded that level in the past, we saw decreased consumption, decreased economic activity, and increased uncertainty. And uncertainty, as I have demonstrated previously, is the biggest enemy of sustained economic growth in any country.

NOTES

1. https://en.wikipedia.org/wiki/Laffer_curve (retrieved in June 2016).
2. Uriel Spiegel and Joseph Templeman, A Non-Singular Peaked Laffer Curve: Debunking the Traditional Laffer Curve, The American Economist, Vol. 48, No. 2 (Fall, 2004), pp. 61–66 (Spiegel and Templeman 2004).
3. For example, new technology was implemented to support the reforms; examples include compulsory e-filing and proprietary software to spot irregularities and trigger tax audits. These audits were outsourced to the private sector. To soften the bureaucratic burden for small businesses, simplified tax keys were introduced, e.g., based on the number of chairs at a barbershop or the number of tables at a restaurant.
4. Defined as a country that has had a "fast growth decade," i.e., a ten-year period during which nominal GDP per capita in terms of purchasing power parity doubled and average real growth was at least 6 percent, based on data from the International Monetary Fund and the World Bank. Oil-exporting countries and countries with the population of less than one million were excluded from the analysis.
5. Revenue consists of taxes, social contributions, grants receivable, and other revenue. Revenue increases government's net worth, which is the difference between its assets and liabilities (GFSM 2001, paragraph 4.20). Note: Transactions that merely change the composition of the balance sheet do not change the net worth position, for example, proceeds from sales of nonfinancial and financial assets or incurrence of liabilities.
6. www.theguardian.com/business/ng-interactive/2015/apr/29/the-austerity-delusion (retrieved in 2015).
7. www.bloomberg.com/news/articles/2015-09-17/greece-hints-at-end-of-europe-s-anti-austerity-revolt (retrieved in Septemebr, 2105).
8. With additional income from privatization and reduction of social subsidies as exceptions.
9. See Chap. 6, Privatizing State-Owned Enterprises, for details.
10. Some experts attribute the obsession with austerity to the "political dominance of financial interests." See, for example, Robert Kuttner, *Debtors' Prison: The Politics of Austerity Versus Possibility*, Knopf, New York 2013 (Kuttner 2013).

11. Georgia was promised special aid from IFIs after the Russian invasion, an important factor that helped uphold national morale and instill confidence in investors. However, the bulk of the funds that IFIs had promised did not actually reach Georgia until late 2010, or even early 2011, when Georgia was already on a path to recovery of its own accord.

12. The best experts in many technical areas are typically employed by private sector companies, often simply because IFIs cannot pay top salaries for political reasons.

13. https://www.bloomberg.com/view/articles/2012-08-20/how-volcker-launched-his-attack-on-inflation (retrieved in May 2016).

14. This slowdown can be further aggravated by the slightly higher costs of loans in a deflationary economy. In an inflationary economy, however, devaluation will eat up part of the loan itself.

CHAPTER 4

Creating a Business-Friendly Climate

Abstract This chapter describes the benefits of the hub economy and tells the story of how Georgia became a hub for regional trade thanks to simplified rules and smart regulations. As its centerpiece, this chapter presents an account of successful Georgian reforms in "Doing Business" areas recognized by the World Bank, such as Georgia jumping from 112th place in 2006 the 8th place in 2014, as well as Georgia being named as the top reformer worldwide for the period of 2006–2011. The chapter provides a first-hand account of how the government changed the mindset of public officials with the introduction of the "one government" principle and rules such as "silence is consent." It concludes with a discussion of the World Bank's ranking methodology and a case example from Kazakhstan, a country that has applied many of the lessons learned in Georgia to create its own road map for reform in 2015–2016.

Keywords Business-friendly · Hub · Simeon Djankov · Piggybacking · One-stop-shop · SME · Silence is Consent · One Government Principle

4.1   The Hub Economy

Georgia is not particularly rich in natural resources. The country is not an oil exporter, and it doesn't mine diamonds or precious metals (except for relatively small amounts of gold). Georgia has always had a high current account deficit, and an inflow of foreign capital has always been vital to sustain the country's economy. In the early 2000s, Georgia was a poor country. It is still not a rich country – a lower-middle economy according to the World Bank classification.[1] But back then, Georgia was among the poorest countries in the world. There were only two prospective sources of substantial growth: local entrepreneurial activity and foreign direct investment.

At the time, in the early 2000s, attracting foreign investment seemed, to put it mildly, challenging. Georgia had a recent history of civil wars, a high criminal rate, and a high level of corruption. The geopolitical situation was not exactly stable; the danger of forcible Russian interference was always looming in the background. On top of all this, the total size of the prize was comparatively small, given Georgia's population of just over four million people and nominal GDP per capita below USD 1000. So why would any investor want to do business in Georgia? Other countries in the region were much more attractive: oil-rich Azerbaijan; Turkey, a newly emerged huge market with a very vibrant economy; Eastern European countries, such as Bulgaria and Romania, which were already members of North Atlantic Treaty Organization (NATO) and would soon become members of the European Union.[2] And still Georgia grew faster than most of its neighbors between 2004 and 2012,[3] and this growth came from foreign investment. Unlikely as it sounds, Georgia found its niche as an attractive environment for private enterprise and foreign investment.

The successful fight against corruption as described in earlier chapters was the most important driver of economic growth. Additionally, the government went to great lengths to create a business-friendly environment – by increasing transparency, reducing the administrative burden for private companies; providing opportunities for entrepreneurial activity; and demonstrating to foreign investors that Georgia was more attractive than its neighbors in terms of regulation, taxation, and business climate. All rules and regulations were reviewed from the point of view of the private sector: what were the obstacles for entrepreneurs? What regulatory problems did investors face? In the first two years after the Rose Revolution, 2004 and 2005, the plan was to liberalize the economy and create a business-friendly environment to attract investment. In 2009 and 2010, these efforts became part of the more comprehensive vision to create a "hub economy." Transforming Georgia as a regional hub for investment, trade, transit, tourism, and education would bring the next wave of growth.

Hubs typically grow faster than their neighbors and manage to develop a more diversified economy that makes them less susceptible to recession than other countries. Their economies are resilient, i.e., less likely to be hit by an economic downturn, and they recover faster than other countries. But location is not enough to qualify as a hub. Governments need to make a real and sustained effort to create a business-friendly environment to take advantage of the benefits of the hub economy.

The main characteristics of the hub economy are:

- A geographical location that makes a country a gateway for other countries.
- An open economy that allows for free trade with most of the region.
- A well-developed transportation infrastructure.
- A low level of corruption.
- An attractive business environment, including low taxation.

Around the world many countries qualify as potential hubs because of their location and geopolitical position. Some of these countries have already realized this potential as a result of purposeful transformations to acquire the characteristics listed previously. Examples of countries that have taken advantage of their location and transformed themselves into regional, or even global, hubs include Singapore and Hong Kong. Many countries are still in the process of transformation.

Georgia is a good example of how a country can start a transformation into a regional hub. In 2010, Georgia's geographical location and natural resources were the same as in the late 1990s. Its geopolitical position was, perhaps, even weaker than it had been before. But economically, the tide had turned. Within a decade, Georgia had transformed itself from a failed state that was close to bankruptcy into a fast-growing, extremely resilient economy. Despite the double blow of the world financial crisis and the Russian invasion, Georgia's economy grew at a rate of 6.7 percent annually over the period from 2003 to 2012 (CAGR). Georgia suffered less from the recession, and recovered more quickly, than any other country in the region.

All this wasn't due to a stroke of good luck. It was the result of the government's dedicated efforts to remake Georgia as a hub. By 2010, Georgia had successfully fought corruption, invested in infrastructure, put in place free trade agreements with all neighboring countries, and significantly improved its business environment. It had turned its geographical position into a source of economic advantage and re-invented itself as a hub.

The benefit of the hub economy becomes most apparent when you look at the development of Georgian exports. In 2004, the most exported type of product was scrap metal, accounting for approximately 16 percent of all exports. In 2010, vehicles topped the list of Georgia's exports – although Georgia had never produced, or even assembled, any vehicles. Rather, the change was driven by simplified rules and regulations, a decrease in corruption, and investments in transportation infrastructure (see the discussion of tax and customs reforms in the next chapter). Because of these improvements, car dealers gladly chose Georgia's open economy as their regional trade center. In Georgia, it was faster and cheaper to import a vehicle, obtain customs clearance, register the vehicle to a buyer, and then re-export it to any other country in the region. Car dealers from almost all over the world brought to Georgia cars destined for the whole region. Azeri, Arminian, and Kazakh car dealers then bought and resold these cars to buyers in their respective countries. Dealers of the used cars followed suit. Before long, Georgia had turned into the regional center for vehicle trading.[4] Tens of thousands of jobs were created, and Georgia's current account deficit was reduced – not by building new factories or new industrial zones but by smart regulations and simple rules.

4.2   Georgia's "Doing Business" Reforms

The benefits of the hub economy are contingent on a business-friendly environment. Georgia's transformation into a business-friendly country started in 2005. The World Bank had just published its first "Ease of Doing Business" report, but our government was still busy getting its house in order after the Rose Revolution. Fighting corruption in government agencies and state-owned enterprises was our top priority at the time. While we were determined to improve Georgia's business climate, the "Doing Business" rating itself was on the margins of our attention at best.

Imagine our surprise when the World Bank contacted us in the fall of 2007 with the news that, thanks to reforms initiated in 2004, Georgia had jumped from 112th to 37th place in the "Doing Business" rating. Because of the magnitude of this improvement, Simeon Djankov, chief economist of the finance and private sector vice-presidency of the World Bank, personally came all the way to Georgia from Washington, D.C. Simeon commended Georgia on its unprecedented success.[5] We thanked him and said that we aspired to break into the top 20. Although he was an admirer of Georgia, Simeon was skeptical. Much to his – and lot of other observers' – surprise, Georgia went on to not only make the top 20, but even the top 10. In 2014, Georgia was ranked 8th. Out of the 10 topics covered by the "Doing Business" Report, Georgia excelled in 5 categories:

- Starting a business
- Registering property
- Dealing with construction permits
- Labor regulations
- Getting credit

In 2011, Georgia was nominated as the number one reformer worldwide for the period from 2006 to 2011. According to the World Bank, no other country has made as many reforms as Georgia to make doing business easier. Although Georgia has since lost its peak ranking, it remains one of the most attractive countries to do business in globally.

So how was it done? How do you move from 112th place to 37th in one year, and from 112th to 8th in less than a decade? You start by introducing the kinds of reforms most civil servants will tell you are "impossible." For example, we abolished the vast majority – about 85 percent – of all pre-existing licenses and permits during the first wave of our efforts to improve the business climate between 2004 and 2006. The impact of these and similar changes was not limited to the "Doing Business" ranking. Rather, the ranking reflected substantial improvements that made a big and tangible difference in the real world. For example, as a direct effect of our reforms, construction in Georgia veritably skyrocketed between 2004 and 2006. The share of construction as a percentage of GDP grew from 6.4 percent in 2004 to 9.0 percent in 2006. Over the course of the same period, the square footage approved for development in Tbilisi increased almost fivefold, from 423,000 m^2 in 2004 to 2,175,000 m^2 in 2006. Land registration saw similar growth rates in these years.

Heartened by such early successes and the World Bank's recognition, the government launched the second and third stages of its reforms to make Georgia more business friendly. We listened to the concerns of private sector players, big and small, and refined many regulations accordingly. Examples of such smart, business-friendly regulatory principles, all but one of which were applied successfully in Georgia, include:

1. One government principle
2. Silence is consent

3. Fee-based service delivery
4. *Ex ante* vs. *ex post* licensing
5. Regulatory guillotine
6. Piggybacking
7. Sunset clause approach

The biggest challenge we faced was to change the mindset of government employees. Every time we – as the new government – tried to introduce an innovative approach, improve the service to the public, simplify the rules, or streamline procedures, we hit a wall of resistance from the very people who worked for us, especially from middle managers in government agencies and other public institutions. "This is how we have always done it," "What you are suggesting is impossible," and "What about public safety?" were their top three retorts. As if public safety was a function of the number of licenses people had to apply for, or the hours they spent standing in line to get a permit! Many reforms were initially delayed by such objections from bureaucrats. They had no reason to welcome any changes. The more permits people had to apply for, and the longer they had to wait to get them, the bigger the opportunity for extortion. What better place is there to solicit a bribe for expedited service than a really long line of frustrated applicants? The old-school bureaucrats didn't care that these practices gave the public service as a whole a bad name. They had nothing to gain or lose from the public image of the government. All they cared about was protecting their income and their influence.

After many discussions, we came up with two overarching principles that helped change the mindset of middle managers in the public service to an astonishing degree: the one government principle and the rule that silence is consent. We made it clear that the state would only succeed or fail as a whole, and that those who were a part of the problem would be fired, while those who made an effort to become part of the solution would be rewarded and rise through the ranks. The "silence is consent" rule creates incentives for public servants to simplify bureaucratic processes, as described later in the text. As these principles gained traction, public servants started approaching members of the government with their own ideas for simplification and improved government services. They had always known which rules were redundant or unnecessarily complex, but they had had no motivation to do anything about it. Reducing or simplifying regulation would have implied reducing their illicit gains. The new rules gave them an incentive to break their habit of self-serving obstruction, and that's why things started to change. The reform of rules and regulations went hand in hand with a reform of the civil service itself. This was an important factor in bringing about a mindset change among civil servants. While the number of civil servants was reduced, the salaries of those who remained increased by a factor of ten or more. As a result, the face of the civil service had changed when the second and third stages of our reforms took effect. It was now a much more qualified, and much more fairly paid, group of people than it had ever been before.

4.2.1   One Government Principle

Nothing is as frustrating for a citizen or an entrepreneur as having to deal with multiple government agencies, and juggle multiple documents and certificates, to get a simple thing done. For example, to register a new company before 2004, the founder had to get registered at the department of statistics and at the tax department, obtain a clean criminal record for the director and owners of the company from the Ministry of the Interior, get an official stamp, get a court order, and so on. Today, registering a new business in Georgia only takes a few minutes, and the registrar will supply the founder with all necessary information, including a bank account number for the new company. We call this the "one government" principle: "A government agency cannot request from a citizen any documents, or any additional information, which is the responsibility of another government agency." The population perceives the government as one entity, and most people don't understand why one government agency would require them to provide it with a stamped paper issued by another government agency. And they are right. Why should a private citizen do the job of the government? In response, Georgia has adapted the one-stop-shop principle for the public administration. Citizens now have to deal with one entity only to obtain any kind of service from the government.

And while many governments have adopted similar one-stop-shopping approaches, sometimes in the shape of single, all-purpose service windows at border crossings or government agencies,[6] Georgia has gone further. We built large public service halls in all major cities, which gather almost all services the government provides to citizens and businesses under one roof. The portfolio includes more than 400 different types of service. You can go there to obtain a birth certificate, pick up a passport, or register a company. The average waiting time is less than three minutes, and the average time it takes to complete a given service is five to six minutes. Services are provided to citizens by specially trained professionals from the office of the government, while the actual administrative work is handled by specialists at the respective ministries, departments, and agencies in back offices. The concept was immediately easy on citizens, but initially hard on officials. They had to give up part of their previous power, and it took a lot of behind-the-scenes coordination to make it work, but the impact was overwhelmingly positive. In a 2010 report, the European Bank for Reconstruction and Development (EBRD) ranked Georgia as the number one country when it comes to official document delivery. And according to a 2012 World Bank survey, 92 percent of citizens were satisfied with how Georgia's public sector issues documents. This was one of the most popular reforms of all, and it helped bring the government the political credit that it needed to introduce further, partly unpopular reforms.

4.2.2   *Silence Is Consent*

Prior to 2006, government agencies took two to three months to answer even a simple query. Applying for a permit, e.g., to build a house or a commercial building, would result in a waiting time of six to nine months. Agencies came up with irrelevant inquiries, or requests for additional information, simply to stall the process. As an applicant, you had no way of knowing whether the approval process was in progress at all, let alone when to expect a definitive answer. In fact, the system was deliberately designed to elicit bribes from applicants: if you paid a bribe, your application would be expedited. People were frustrated, and many stopped applying for permits and licenses altogether. The country as a whole paid the price for these practices, simply because so much entrepreneurial energy went to waste and much of the economic activity was conducted in the shadows. In 2007, we introduced a 30-day deadline for all license applications (20 days for permits). If you apply for a license now and don't hear back from the government within 30 days, the application is considered approved for all intents and purposes.

In practice, making the "silence is consent" principle work smoothly requires some administrative precautions:

- In many cases, an applicant still needs some sort of certificate or signed paper for the record. So even if the applicant is entitled to assume an affirmative answer after the deadline expires, they will still lack the corresponding documentation. To fix this, you need some sort of high-level authority that is entitled to issue the documentation in question. In Georgia, such an authority was not created. As a result, these incidents are handled by the courts, which have the power to force the respective agency to issue proper documentation with the required approval, although this power has never been exercised to date.
- Agencies still tend to come up with all sorts of irrelevant inquiries and questions to justify an extension of the deadline. This tendency undermines the entire "silence is consent" concept and lets the old regime of constant delays creep back in. We introduced specific regulation to keep such delays at bay. When an agency asks for additional information, which it is entitled to do only once according to the new rules, the clock restarts as soon as the missing information is supplied by the applicant.

Thanks to "one government" and "silence is consent," civil servants now think differently about how they provide services to the public. In the past, civil servants did not care how many different types of documents an applicant, be it a citizen or a company, had to submit to obtain a given license or permit, nor did they care how many different agencies the applicant had to deal with for a single application. After the reform, things changed. As one-stop service providers, civil servants were now responsible for collecting all required documents themselves, and inaction would lead to automatic approval of an application. Suddenly, officials personally felt the pain of unnecessarily complex rules and regulations. Initially, they were still reluctant to introduce simplifications that would make one of their colleagues redundant, or simply reduce someone's perceived or actual authority and importance. But the new regulations ("silence is consent" and "one government" principle), put together, made it clear that their own job security was contingent on their contribution to a more efficient administration. Once civil servants realized that the role of government had changed, and that they could be fired if they didn't play along, they started looking at rules and regulations from a new angle. Before, officials treated citizens as petitioners. Now, the customer is king.

4.2.3   Fee-Based Service Delivery

Improving the quality and the efficiency of services provided to the public, as well as the attitude of those providing the services, is one of the most important objectives that any government can set out to achieve. This is so important because all citizens eventually have to deal with a government agency, because citizens pay for the salaries of civil servants through their taxes and because the government has a monopoly on many services. A citizen cannot turn to a private company, after all, to get a passport or register a business. A government that manages to have its agencies provide such services in a reliable, fast, and courteous manner will be richly rewarded with the gratitude and the future favor of the electorate.

In the late 1990s, people stood in line for hours, sometimes for days, at Georgia's government agencies to get a passport, register property, or register a business. In fact, civil servants purposefully made sure that waiting times were long and frustrating to elicit bribes from applicants who wanted – or needed – to skip the line. For so-called "commercial clients," it made all the sense in the world to pay these bribes, rather than to leave their businesses unattended while they stood in line. In our fight against corruption, we increased the salaries of civil servants, recruited new people, and re-organized the way agencies provided services to citizens (see above for details). But of course, sometimes lines would form nevertheless, and there was still demand for extra-fast services.

Before corrupt practices could take root again, we simply decided to legalize the system of charging money for expedited service. What once was a bribe would now be an official fee. The basic service, whatever it was, would be free or carry only a small fee to cover the cost. For example, obtaining a new passport would normally take two weeks and cost only what it took to produce and deliver the document. But if you needed it faster, you would have to pay an extra fee – the faster, the costlier, e.g., USD 100 for delivery within 24 hours and USD 250 for delivery within one hour. As a general rule, however, the basic service itself had to be reasonably fast and free (or adequately priced), and only those who needed accelerated service would pay an extra fee. This was to avoid a scenario in which civil servants charged everyone the extra fee.

As an additional incentive for civil servants to act in a customer-friendly fashion, the extra fees for faster service partially went to the bonuses for the employees of the agency providing the service. This was the only exception to the "one budget" principle discussed previously. It applied only to agencies that had direct interaction with the public, and it helped increase the service orientation of these agencies.

4.2.4   Ex Ante *vs.* Ex Post *Licensing*

Traditionally, you have to apply for a license before you can start a business (*ex ante*), e.g., to open a restaurant. At the same time, you have to get your ducks in a row as an entrepreneur – secure financing, enter into contracts with suppliers, buy equipment, hire staff, get insurance, and so on. Now assume the license is denied. All your efforts will have been in vain, and you will never be able to recover your upfront investment. Your future as a restaurateur is contingent on a check-up by the respective regulator before you earn your first dollar. In many cases, the inspector will not show up for days, or even weeks, while you pace the dining area like a cat on a hot tin roof. And when the inspector finally comes by, the opening may be further delayed because of some minor issue that you could well have taken care of during operations, such as installing air conditioning or adding a second restroom. The same inspector will return after the opening, typically once a year, but subsequent inspections will not be as meticulous as the first one.

Now imagine you didn't need a license at all, or – if you did need it – could apply for it while you were already serving guests at your new restaurant and generating revenue. Why shouldn't it be that way? In fact, I believe that most businesses do not need any licensing. Why should a small retail shop, or a hairdresser, have to apply for a license at all? Of course, there are some exceptions, especially in areas that concern the health and safety of the public. But even in most of those cases, I believe that licensing could happen in parallel to operations (*ex post*). As a restaurateur, you could open your restaurant whenever you were ready. You would have to expect an inspector to come by any time, though, to make sure you adhere to all applicable health and safety regulations. You would not forego any revenue (especially during the first months of operations when the initially generated revenue is so important for an entrepreneur) because of delays prior to the opening, and you would be motivated to take extra care to serve only fresh food, keep the place clean, provide impeccable service, and only employ staff that have the proper papers – because there is no telling when there might be an inspection. The most important aspect of switching from *ex ante* to *ex post* licensing is the reduced bargaining power of the inspector. When it is up to an inspector to decide whether or not to allow a newly built (or renovated) commercial entity to operate, the inspector has significant power over the entrepreneur and is in a position to request a bribe or make other unreasonable requests. But once a commercial entity is operational, it becomes more difficult to close it down based on bogus claims.

Critics say that, in an *ex post* environment, a guest at a restaurant might suffer from food poisoning before the first inspection takes place. But who says that this couldn't happen in an *ex ante* environment, despite the pre-opening inspection? A restaurant that is spotless today might still serve spoilt food tomorrow. There is no such thing as 100 percent safety, not even with *ex ante* licensing. In fact, our experience in Georgia indicates that *ex post* licensing is more effective for driving compliance with applicable regulation than *ex ante* licensing. In an *ex ante* environment, companies often let things slide once they have gone through the initial inspection. In an *ex post* environment, companies are always on their guard because an inspector could show up at any time.

4.2.5   Piggybacking

In many developing countries, consumer protection and public safety are used as pretexts to create artificial oligopolies and fill the pockets of a few at the expense of the economy as a whole. These effects were in evidence in Georgia's pharmaceutical industry before the reform of the regulation that governs the introduction of new drugs. The approval process for new drugs was so costly, and so complex, that only three companies were able to shoulder the financial burden in most cases. The sales of these three companies accounted for about three-quarters of all drug sales in Georgia.[7]

To help reduce the threshold for smaller players and increase competition, Georgia decided to take advantage of the expertise developed – and the experience gathered – elsewhere in the world, i.e., to piggyback on other countries' institutions, instead of trying to re-invent the wheel. The pharmaceutical industry is well suited to piggybacking since many regulatory requirements are essentially the same, or very similar, in all countries, regardless of regional differences.

Before the introduction of piggybacking, new drugs had to go through an extensive inspection process before they could be sold on the Georgian market: Is the drug safe? Does it do what it is supposed to do? What are the side effects? Answering these questions was – and still is – a very long and cumbersome process. It requires sophisticated laboratories and well-trained, professionals to see it through. However, if the drug in question is an internationally approved pharmaceutical product, it will already have gone through this process elsewhere, and the manufacturer will already have provided the answers to the relevant agencies in the respective countries. So why do it again? The only question that remains is which countries can be trusted to be sufficiently meticulous to accept their approval as reliable. In Georgia, the government decided that if a drug is approved for use in the European Union, the United States, Japan, Australia, or New Zealand, it would automatically also receive approval for use in Georgia. This is because the Georgian authorities realized that the respective agencies in those countries were better equipped than their counterparts in Georgia, and that their experts were much more experienced than their Georgian peers. The underlying assumption was that the relevant health authorities of these countries would take good care to protect their citizens from unsafe drugs, and that Georgia could, hence, trust their ruling.

Piggybacking on pre-existing foreign drug regulations significantly sped up the process of introducing and importing new drugs to Georgia. It also increased the intensity of competition among manufacturers and helped break up the *de facto* oligopoly. Today, all drugs that have already been approved in the European Union, the United States, Japan, Australia, or New Zealand can be sold in Georgia (only the relevant instructions need to be translated into Georgian language). According to a recent study, the number of drugs registered increased by 94 percent, and prices decreased by up to 30 percent, within one year of the introduction of piggybacking in 2010: "We found consistent evidence that the adoption of the approval and reporting regimes had a statistically and quantitatively significant downward effect on drug prices in Georgia. [...] The regulatory reforms [...] in Georgia must be counted as a success."[8] Today, Georgia is one of the first markets to which new drugs can be introduced once they are approved either by health boards in the countries mentioned previously. Similar approaches were applied to construction materials and other products that require a high degree of technological sophistication, and a lot of time, to check and approve.

4.2.6   Regulatory Guillotine

In many countries, legacy regulation is substantial. Much of this regulation is out of date and doesn't add value any longer. Yet it still causes a lot of bureaucratic effort to enforce and oversee, and it provides officials with plenty of opportunity to make the lives of citizens more difficult than they should be, or would have to be. Yet many governments have tried in vain to weed out superfluous regulations. As soon as the government tries to get rid of such regulation, some part of the administrative apparatus will advance an argument why it is necessary to keep it. This is because complex regulation is a job guarantee for civil servants. In fact, this is often the only purpose it serves. The burden of proof is on the reformist government. But how do you demonstrate to an army of veteran bureaucrats that the regulation that they have spent decades developing, refining, and defending is not needed anymore?

This is exactly the predicament the Georgian government found itself in after the Rose Revolution. We wanted to reduce the state's regulatory footprint to set the economy free. But every time we tried to eliminate useless regulations, some agency or middle manager would protest and ask us to prove that the new approach was better. In some cases we succeeded, but in some we didn't. The breakthrough came in 2005 when the government turned the tables on the bureaucrats. We announced that all regulation would be annulled in certain sectors – unless the relevant agencies could prove within a certain period that a particular piece of regulation was necessary to protect the health and safety of the population, and that the regulation was actually used in practice, and for purposes other than corruption. This approach, sometimes referred to as a "regulatory guillotine," helped us eliminate countless petty rules and reduce the number of licenses and permits by 85 percent.

4.2.7   Sunset Clause Approach

The idea of the sunset clause approach is to attach an expiry date to those rules and regulations that deal with a temporary issue in a particular context. It is based on the experience that such regulation will eventually become obsolete. According to this approach, regulation is automatically revoked after a certain period of time – unless the government or relevant authority expressly renews or prolongs it. In Georgia, this approach was never introduced. In retrospect, however, I believe it would have been beneficial to do so, because the sunset clause approach forces the administration to adjust and update rules and regulations continuously. What is more, it allows the government to get rid of superfluous regulation without any need for specific legislation or other procedures, such as the regulatory guillotine described previously.

4.3   Thoughts on the World Bank's Methodology

Officials everywhere are in the habit of doubting the methodology of the World Bank's "Doing Business" ranking. I have yet to meet a government that doesn't accuse the World Bank of misrepresenting the reality of their country in its ranking. But in my experience, the World Bank is almost always right. Those who doubt the methodology are usually trying to blame the poor performance of their country on someone else, often with the help of a few handpicked examples, many of which are dubious or taken out of context. In reality, the World Bank does not rank countries based on theoretical calculations or unrealistic assumptions, as many of its critics claim. Rather, it collects its information mainly from private companies that have firsthand experience of the public service in question. Indicators are derived from real-life data and compared with the respective results in other countries to create the ranking. Typically, the World Bank combines a *de jure* and a *de facto* perspective:

- Are the written laws and regulations clear and straightforward?
- Are these laws and regulations actually applied in practice?

The World Bank will credit a country with improvements only if both questions can reliably be answered in the affirmative. For example, Georgia formally introduced its electronic tax filing system as early as 2009. The World Bank, however, did not reflect this reform in the "Doing Business" report until 2011 because the majority of taxpayers did not use the system in the preceding years (see the next chapter for details). In another case, the World Bank did not – initially – credit Georgia with the protection of minority investors. While the actual legal practice was investor-friendly, the written laws were not. The question was whether a minority shareholder suing a partner for wrongdoing could obtain some specific information during the trial, and whether the plaintiff needed to provide a detailed list of documents to obtain all relevant information. In practice, all relevant information was made available to the plaintiff upon request, even if the plaintiff did not name all the documents individually. But the written law gave the courts the power to refuse such a request. Only when we changed the law to conform with the actual practice, clearly stating the obligation of the court to provide all relevant information to the plaintiff, did the World Bank acknowledge the practice. Another example of the same principle related to the enforcement of contracts. The issue was whether a plaintiff could obtain pre-trial attachment of a defendant's movable assets if there was reason to believe that the defendant might try to move these assets out of the court's jurisdiction. The practice was clear – it was possible. However, the written law failed to specify some of the details of the process, which is why the practice was not fully reflected in the World Bank's report. Although many readers may think that these examples are of minor importance, the ability to rely on such regulations can make all the difference for small and medium-sized enterprises (SMEs).

By and large, the regulatory burden a government puts on the economy is well reflected by the World Bank's reports. Of course, like any such report, it cannot be 100 percent accurate. But I am convinced that it gives a very good indication of a country's business environment. The report takes into account many of the practical factors that determine whether it is sufficiently easy to do business for an existing local SME, or whether a potential foreign investor will even consider entering a given market. Examples include:

- How much money do you need to start a business?
- What does it cost to obtain a construction permit?
- How long does it take to register property?

In some of the countries I have visited as an advisor, it can take an investor up to two years to get ready to start a company – registering the business, getting a permit for the construction of a warehouse, registering property, and getting connected to the nearest electricity grid. Representatives of the World Bank collect all such information, mostly from private sector players who have first-hand experience of the procedures in question. These companies know how long a given process actually takes, rather than how long it is supposed to take, and how much it actually costs to get a given permit, rather than how much it is supposed to cost, i.e., whether they have to pay a bribe to get it done. Such first-hand information makes the report a valuable source for everyone contemplating to do business in a given country. In São Paolo, Brazil, for example, obtaining a construction permit legally takes 425 days, on average. Indirectly, this kind of information also serves as an indicator of potential corruption. If the legal process takes 425 days, chances are that most investors will be willing to pay a bribe to speed it up. Last, but not least, governments that have their mindset on reforms can use the report as a roadmap to reduce the regulatory burden and remove bureaucratic bottlenecks that hinder economic growth.

In Georgia, there is a clear correlation between the "Doing Business" ranking and actual business activity. As Georgia's rank improved from 112th to 8th, the number of SMEs registered per year more than quadrupled in the period from 2004 to 2013.

The experience in other countries is similar, and empirical studies confirm that the "Doing Business" ranking correlates with actual economic performance:

- High-ranked countries grow faster than lower-ranked countries. On average, the countries in the top quartile of the report show 2.3 percent higher economic growth than those in the bottom quartile.[9]
- On average, each day of delay for exports and imports reduces international trade by 1 percent.[10]
- A 10 percent reduction in tax complexity is comparable to a 1 percent reduction in effective corporate tax rates in terms of its effect on foreign direct investment.[11]
- Cutting the number of procedures required to start a business in half is associated with a 14 percent increase in the number of new business registrations. A similar reduction of the number of days required to register a business is linked to a 19 percent increase, while an equivalent cut in the cost is associated with a 30 percent increase.[12]

None of these reforms is easy to pull off, but they are worth the effort. If the political will is there, effective coordination is in place, and those responsible have a good understanding of the topic, they can be pushed through quickly, and to great public acclaim. For example, the introduction of public service halls in Georgia described previously was immensely popular with citizens and gave the government credit to make other, less popular changes that were necessary to get Georgia back on track.

I encourage governments of developing countries everywhere to embark on an ambitious journey to improve the local business climate substantially and sustainably, as we have done in Georgia. If they succeed, any respectable rating will show it.

4.4   "DOING BUSINESS" REFORMS IN KAZAKHSTAN

In April 2014, Karim Massimov was re-approved as prime minister of Kazakhstan. We had both served as prime ministers of our countries before, become friends, and both left office in 2012. I gave him a call in May 2014, a few weeks after he had been nominated again by the president and was re-confirmed as prime minister by the parliament.

"Congratulations, Mr. Prime Minister," I said.

"Hello, Mr. Prime Minister. How have you been?", he replied.

"Unlike you, Mr. Prime Minister, I am retired," I said.

"Once a prime minister, always a prime minister. It's one of those titles that stay with you for life," Karim insisted.

We both laughed.

"Listen, Nika, why don't you come to Astana? It would be great to see you again and catch up," he said.

"Great. Will do. Again, congratulations!"

A few days later, we were having tea at his office. Prime Minister told me that Kazakhstan wanted to diversify its oil-based economy and accelerate its business climate reforms. He also said that the government was determined to initiate the necessary changes but that his team might need some help to pull the right levers. It was a great opportunity for me to show that the reforms described in this book were not only applicable to a small country like Georgia, but to other, bigger countries like Kazakhstan as well.

"So what are you doing these days, Nika?" he asked.

"As it happens, I am writing a book about the reforms in Georgia. I also advise some other governments in the region to help them apply the lessons we learned in Georgia. And I have some ideas for great reforms that we never got round to implementing in Georgia, but that other countries might benefit from."

"Listen, why don't you help us with the 'Doing Business' reforms? We can discuss some other reforms too, both those you made in Georgia and the ones that you wanted to make in Georgia, but could not."

"Sounds great," I said.

"Why don't you study our situation and come back with some new ideas for reforms? We'll take your advice, and then you can put the story in your book. You can call the chapter 'Reforms that I was not able to implement in Georgia, but that were passed in Kazakhstan with the help of my friend, the prime minister of Kazakhstan'."

He had a big smile on his face. I loved his proposal. At the time, I had just started my advisory firm and was looking for a reformist government that had the political will to change. It would be a great opportunity to put both the applicability of the reforms and my own capability as an advisor to the test. Prime minister introduced to me his deputy, Mr. Bakytzhan Sagintaev, saying that Bakytzhan would lead the reforms. I sat down with Mr. Sagintayev and explained to him the Georgian reforms, the methodology of the "Doing Business" report, and the changes in legislation and regulation that we had introduced in Georgia. I also spent some time describing the main obstacles that we had had to overcome along the way.

"The biggest problem will be your own staff – deputy ministers, heads of agencies, maybe even some ministers. Most of them won't like the reforms," I said.

"This won't be an issue. Our plan was approved at the highest level. We will see this through. You tell me what it takes, and I will make it happen," he replied.

"Very well. Let's stay in touch," I said.

"Absolutely," he confirmed.

I said my goodbyes and headed to the airport.

A few days later deputy prime minister called me.

"Nika, I have met with the heads of agencies and deputy ministers who would have to implement the reforms we discussed. I explained to them what needs to be done. Guess what their response was."

"I have a hunch that they didn't like your agenda."

"They said 'It's impossible,' exactly as you predicted."

"I'm not surprised. There is an almost natural selection process that brings people who treasure stability, and despise change, into these positions. If you are a risk-taker, you start a business. If you prefer to play it safe, you become a civil servant."

"Let's prove them wrong."

"It will be my privilege."

We worked together over the course of the next 2 years. More than 130 changes to laws, rules, and regulations were introduced in during the first year alone. In 2015 Kazakhstan was nominated as a number one reformer worldwide for that year. The country jumped from 77th to 41st in the "Doing Business" ranking from one year to the next. The World Bank acknowledged 19 reforms in 7 areas out of the 10 that it monitors: starting a business, dealing with permits, registering property, getting credit, protecting minority investors, enforcing contracts, and resolving insolvency.[13,14] Kazakhstan became the country that introduced the highest number of reforms in any one year since the World Bank's "Ease of Doing Business" report was first published. A year later Kazakhstan advanced to become 35th in the ranking and this time 18 reforms in 7 areas were aknowledged by the World Bank. Kazakhstan was also nominated as the second biggest reformer of the year and among top three countries that made the most reforms since 2004 (after Georgia and Macedonia).

Thanks to these reforms, Kazakhstan is reducing its dependence on oil, creating a structural advantage over its neighbors, and evolving into a regional hub for trade and investment. More generally, Kazakhstan is a good example of how one country can take inspiration from reforms made in another country, even if the two countries are different in terms of their economic development and geopolitical position, provided the government is determined to create a more business-friendly environment and promote economic growth driven by private enterprise.

NOTES

1. http://data.worldbank.org/country/georgia (retrieved in June 2016).
2. Bulgaria and Romania joined the EU in 2007; see http://europa.eu/about-eu/countries/member-countries/index_de.htm (retrieved in June 2016).
3. Thanks to oil exports, Azerbaijan grew even faster than Georgia.

4. See the description of special customs zones in the Chapter on "Reforming Taxes and Customs."

5. To this day, no other country has seen a bigger year-on-year improvement.

6. See http://unpan1.un.org/intradoc/groups/public/documents/ UNECE/UNPAN019892.pdf (retrieved in May 2016).

7. Steve H. Hanke, Alexander B. Rose, Stephen J.K. Walters, *How to make medicine safe and cheap*, Health and Medicine, Fall 2014 (Hanke et al. 2014).

8. Cato Institute. See Steve H. Hanke, Alexander B. Rose, Stephen J. K. Walters, *How to make medicine safe and cheap*, Health and Medicine, Fall 2014 (Hanke et al. 2014).

9. Djankov, McLiesh, Ramalho – 2006, Djankov and Pham – 2010, Lawless – 2013.

10. Djankov, Freund, and Pham, 2010

11. Lawless, 2013.

12. Lawless, 2013.

13. http://www.doingbusiness.org/reforms/top-reformers-2016 (retrieved in May 2016).

14. "Ease of Doing Business 2017" report of the World Bank – pg. 8 and 25.

CHAPTER 5

Reforming Taxes and Customs

Abstract This chapter describes how Georgia's government ended the rule of the shadow economy with the help of tax and customs reforms. The key was simplicity. The number of general taxes was cut from 21 to 6, all of them low, flat, and simple, and despite this action tax collections increased tenfold in the period of nine years (2003–2011) in nominal terms and from 7 to 24 percent in terms of percent to GDP. The number of customs duties was reduced from 16 to 3. More than 90 percent of all imported goods were allowed into the country without any customs duty, making Georgia one of the most open economies in the region. The author also outlines some innovative approaches to tax administration such as outsourcing of tax audits to private sector, using lottery for improved tax compliance, etc. The chapter concludes with a discussion of the Estonian model of profit taxation.

Keywords Roadshow · E-filing · Mediation · Ombudsman · Prime Minister

In 2004, Georgia's government set out to end the rule of the shadow economy that had brought the country to the brink of bankruptcy. Specifically, the government vowed to create a transparent system of rules that would spur on both domestic entrepreneurship and foreign investment. The key was simplicity. The number of general taxes was cut from 21 to 7. The number of customs duties was reduced from 16 to 3. More than 90 percent of all imported goods were allowed into the country without any customs duty, making Georgia one of the most open economies in the region. New technology was introduced to improve tax and customs administrations; examples include compulsory e-filing of tax returns and proprietary software to spot irregularities and trigger tax audits. To ease the bureaucratic burden for small businesses, simplified tax keys were introduced, e.g., based on the number of chairs at a barbershop or the number of tables at a restaurant.

5.1   TAX CODE SIMPLIFICATION

Reducing both the number of taxes and the tax rate led to a significant boost in tax revenues; see Chap. 3, Rightsizing Fiscal and Monetary Policies. These policies were the most visible elements of our tax reform, but they constituted only a small part of a much larger package of legal and administrative improvements. Our mission was to introduce any change that would help reduce corruption. Cleaning up the tax department itself – laying off people, recruiting new specialists – was an important step, but it was not enough. Like most developing countries, Georgia suffered from a lack of high-caliber tax professionals, and most of the really good ones were employed by the private sector, where wages were much higher than in the tax department. As a result, the talent pool for tax auditors was frightfully small. We were afraid that auditors would jump at any chance to take advantage of ambiguity and bend the rules in favor of those who were willing to pay for it. To prevent this from happening, we made the rules as simple and transparent as possible, leaving no room for interpretation. This made the system largely immune to abuse, and it enabled even a small team of auditors to enforce it. It worked. In a survey conducted by Transparency International ("Global Corruption Barometer") in 2012, 0 percent of respondents said that they had paid a bribe to the tax department (Fig. 5.1).[1]

In 2004, Georgia introduced its new tax code, decreasing the number of taxes from 21 to 7 (and to 6 a year later). All taxes were flat and low. There was no incentive to make one's income appear lower than it really was to get into a lower tax bracket. The income tax rate was 25 percent for everybody. In 2009, it was decreased to 20 percent. The profit tax rate was 15 percent, the dividend tax rate 5 percent, the VAT rate was 18 percent, and the property tax rate was up to 1 percent, depending on the local authorities.

According to Tax Code of Georgia	Year 1997	Rate	Year 2004	Rate	Year 2010	Rate
State taxes	1) Income tax	12–20%	1) Income tax	15%	1) Income tax	20%
	2) Profit tax	20%	2) Profit tax	15%	2) Profit tax	15%
	3) VAT	20%	3) VAT	18%	3) VAT	18%
	4) Excise	Various	4) Excise	Various	4) Excise	Various
	5) Property tax	0,5 GEL sq.	5) Import tax	0–5–12%	5) Import tax	0–5–12%
	6) Social insurance tax	31%	6) Social tax	20%		
	7) Property tansfer tax	2%				
	8) Vehicle tax	5–100 GEL				
	9) Natural resource tax	1–35%				
	10) Environment tax	1–450K GEL				
	11) Tax on transport entry on the territory and overload tax	60–880 GEL				
	12) Flat tax	10–90 GEL				
	13) Small business tax	5%				
Local taxes	14) Tax for business activities	1–2%	7) Property tax	1%	6) Property tax	1%
	15) Gambling tax	200 GEL-20%				
	16) Recreational tax	10 GEL p.p.				
	17) Hotel tax	2%				
	18) Advertisement tax	10%				
	19) Tax for using local symbols	2%				
	20) Land tax	2-114 GEL p. ha.				
	21) Parking tax	0,3 GEL – 20%				

Fig. 5.1 Number and types of taxes in Georgia. (*Source:* Law of Georgian on Tax Code, adopted 13/06/1997 and 22/12/2004)

The social tax was abolished as part of the one budget principle that gives the government freedom to use tax revenue as needed, i.e., without earmarking, regardless of its source. In 2011, the government introduced a special tax for SMEs, merging all duties into one to reduce the administrative burden. SMEs could not afford accountants, which is why even the simplified new tax code was still too difficult for them. To make their lives as easy as possible, the merged revenue tax was calculated based on variables that reflected the respective type of business. Examples include:

- Number of beds for small bed and breakfast establishments
- Number of chairs for barber shops
- Number of tables for small restaurants

For small traders and retailers, the merged revenue tax was calculated as a percentage of total revenue. The simplifications helped make tax compliance the new normal. For the first time in Georgia's recent history, everybody contributed.

5.2   MEDIATION

One of the biggest sources of debate and disagreement among the members of the government was the treatment of the private sector by the public prosecutor's office. During the first wave of our reforms (2004–2007), it had been important to take a strong stance on tax issues and make sure that everybody paid fully, especially given the reduced number of taxes and the reduced tax rates. However, the prosecutor's office upheld its pressure on businesses past this period. While this practice did not add much value in terms of tax revenue, it increasingly prompted the hostility of business owners toward the government, sometimes rightfully so. I was part of a group within the government that did its best to reduce the pressure on businesses and ensure they were given fair treatment by the authorities. To this end, we introduced the Internal Dispute Resolution Mechanism (IDRM), a two-round mediation approach. The first round of mediation was conducted by the revenue service itself. If the first round did not bring resolution, the dispute went to the Ministry of Finance. The IDRM panel consisted of the top tax specialists at the Ministry of Finance and of selected members of parliament.

While the IDRM wasn't perfect, it was still the fastest and fairest tool to resolve disputes between the tax department and the private sector. It also helped improve the performance of tax auditors. This was because the auditors had to defend their rulings in front of the highly qualified, very well-paid tax specialists that represented private companies in disputes. Additionally, the IDRM helped us put the finger on flaws in the tax code. In disputes between private sector lawyers and tax department auditors, it often turned out that both parties were right – from a legal perspective. The issue was rooted in the regulation itself – it was unclear or ambiguous, and could be interpreted in two or more ways. In some cases, changes to the tax code were introduced as a result of such findings. For the most part, the ruling of the IDRM was designated as a precedent-setting public ruling, i.e., it was to be applied in all similar cases in the future.

Another institution that was created to protect the private sector from potential abuse was the office of the business ombudsman. The ombudsman was tasked with acting as a mediator between the private sector and the government – not only regarding tax disputes, but other issues as well, such as licensing, permits, privatization, and registration of businesses. The job of the ombudsman was to identify any such contentious issues the private sector – mostly SMEs – might have with specific government agencies, give timely information to the Prime Minister's Office, create an efficient channel of communication, and play the role of a mediator before things got out of hand.

5.3   IT-Enabled Risk Assessment and Outsourcing of Audits

Mediation revealed many problems and inefficiencies in the tax department. The biggest problem was the lack of human resources. Although salaries were not low, good tax auditors were hard to find. And although some of the country's best tax specialists worked for the Ministry of Finance, their capacity was insufficient to monitor and enforce tax compliance as broadly as it was deemed necessary. In response, we introduced an IT-based risk assessment to spot tax violations and decided to outsource some of the functions of the tax department.

The risk assessment tool was a software we had developed in-house. It compared financial data filed by companies of similar size operating in the same industry, identified outliers, and detected implausible entries. This scan was based on parameters such as revenue, profit margin, average salaries of employees, changes in revenue and profit, and other indicators. If any of these figures was at odds with those of other enterprises in the same industry, the system would detect the anomaly immediately. In effect, we had put in place a pattern recognition solution fueled by big data before either term became popular. We made it a rule of thumb to conduct 80–90 percent of all tax audits based on the IT system. Only 10–20 percent of audits were triggered by the head of the tax department. The objective was to conduct all audits based on the tool and thereby eventually eliminate any opportunity for the tax department, or the financial police, to abuse their power.

The IT-based risk assessment was aided by the introduction of compulsory e-filing,[2] a measure that, in and of itself, played a major role in decreasing Georgia's shadow economy. Initially, e-filing was introduced for large companies only. The objective was to minimize interaction between taxpayers and the tax department to leave less room for manipulation and corrupt deals. But when e-filing was launched for all companies, only 5 percent chose to use it. Apparently, taxpayers didn't believe that electronic filing was sufficient. What is more, accountants were reluctant to give up their position of power as intermediaries between taxpayers and the tax department. Although the government ran a dedicated communication campaign, the e-filing system was not gaining sufficient traction. Eventually, the government had to disallow any paper-based tax returns. Ever since, all tax returns in Georgia have been filed electronically.

To increase the tax department's coverage of the economy and make the lives of taxpayers easier, the government decided to outsource some functions of the tax department in 2011 – a highly innovative measure at the time. The Ministry of Finance identified ten private tax-auditing companies and gave them a special license to conduct audits of private companies on behalf of the tax department.[3] If a private company was up for an audit, the company in question would propose one of the ten licensed private auditors to the Ministry of Finance; any auditing firm that had recently provided services to the auditee would not be admitted. The ministry would check if there was any danger of a conflict of interest. If it found that there wasn't, the ministry would authorize the private auditor to represent the revenue service and audit the company on behalf of the tax department. All licensed private auditors were subject to random double checks. If any irregularities were found, the license would be annulled. Once a private enterprise had been notified in writing that an audit by the tax department itself was imminent, this enterprise could no longer choose to be audited by a licensed private auditor. This was to encourage companies to apply for private audits before they had even been earmarked for checks by the government. When a private auditor had completed an audit, the auditee could challenge the rulings through IDRM overseen by the Ministry of Finance. In these cases, the private sector's best tax specialists would take up the issue with their peers – one group acting on behalf of the audited company, the other on behalf of the licensed private tax auditor. The final decision was up to the Ministry of Finance. It was a win-win-win approach:

- Private sector companies gladly paid to be audited by licensed private auditors, rather than by public auditors. This was because the tax department's auditors were often perceived as bossy and interfered with business operations during an audit, while private auditors were typically more sympathetic to the needs of auditees to run their businesses.
- Licensed private auditors were happy to have found a new source of income, and they had little reason to put this substantial revenue stream in jeopardy by accepting bribes from auditees in exchange for favorable audits.
- The Ministry of Finance achieved its goal of covering a much bigger part of the economy, and increase tax compliance, despite its limited resources. As a side benefit, the quality of IDRM debates greatly increased because high-caliber experts were now involved on both sides.

5.4   ADDITIONAL MEASURES

Other measures introduced or envisioned by the government to fight corruption, increase tax compliance, and create a more business-friendly environment included mystery shopping, lotteries on receipts and credit card payments, and electronic tracking and tracing of selected goods, such as cigarettes and alcoholic beverages.

5.4.1   Mystery Shopping

To make sure that all shops and commercial entities conducted their business on the record, used registers, and gave out receipts, the tax department employed mystery shoppers.[4] But since there were only a few of these mystery shoppers, it didn't take long until they were all known to, and recognized by, owners of local shops and restaurants. The authorities decided to recruit private mystery shoppers who were trained by the tax department to act on its behalf. These private mystery shoppers did not receive a base salary, but were paid based only on the penalties that they imposed on commercial entities found to be in violation of the tax code. The approach was quite successful for a while, and it helped to reduce the size of the shadow economy. After a few months, however, private mystery shoppers became too aggressive and started taking advantage even of honest business owners. The mystery shopping approach had served its purpose, and the government decided to discontinue it before it could get out of hand.

5.4.2 *Lottery on Receipts*

Shopkeepers and other small commercial entities are always tempted to keep at least a part of their business off the record, i.e., to hide some of their income from the tax department. An easy way to help them resist this temptation is to have shoppers ask for receipts. But how do you get shoppers to do that? By giving them a reward, or at least the prospect of a reward. To take advantage of this disciplinary effect, we introduced a lottery on receipts for cash transactions. Every week, dozens of winners of cash prizes would be drawn, and the results would be widely publicized. The effect was significant. Reported revenue went up every month. After nine months, the increase started to level off, but reported revenue remained high. Originally, the plan was to introduce a similar kind of lottery for credit card payments to cover an even bigger part of the economy and stimulate wider usage of credit cards, which would have helped decrease the size of the cash-based shadow economy. This second stage, however, was never implemented, although preliminary research showed that it would probably have been successful.

5.4.3 *Electronic Tracking and Tracing*

Excised goods, such as cigarettes and alcohol, are naturally elusive. They have a tendency to disappear off the radar of the authorities and change hands as part of the tax-free shadow economy. To counter this tendency and increase legitimate tax revenue, Georgia introduced an Electronic Tracking and Tracing Mechanism (ETTM) for such goods. In cooperation with a foreign private investor, we set up a system that would cover the entire supply chain from manufacturing to retail.

By the time a given product was made, it had already been assigned a code that was transmitted to the tax department. When the product was put in a box, that box was also marked electronically. The same was true for the van that was used for transportation and its destination, i.e., the particular commercial entity to which the product was delivered for sale. All codes and markings were electronically transmitted to the tax department. Now all a tax inspector had to do was to go to any of the shops and check which products actually belonged there and which ones did not, using an electronic read-out device. The inspector would proceed to investigate the origin, and intended destination, of any product that was found in a store where it didn't belong to pinpoint the perpetrator. To avoid any corrupt deals between inspectors and shopkeepers, the devices inspectors carried were equipped with GPS. That way, the head of tax inspection knew which shop was visited by which employee. The next day, the same store would be visited by a different inspector to double-check the results of the previous day. If any of the shops that had already been inspected was found to stock unregistered goods, the initial inspector was subject to an investigation on charges of corruption and let go if found guilty.

There are many solutions available to track and trace goods in this manner. What set the particular technology we used apart from other solutions was that it assigned and applied electronic markings before a given product was even finished. This made it impossible for the producer to divert part of the production to the black market. This was a key feature. Often, the shipping of goods from factories or warehouses to retailers is the weakest link in the supply chain as far as transparency is concerned. Once the goods enter the retail network, it is very difficult to single out illegitimate batches. When some manufacturers found out about our plans to introduce ETTM, they started to increase their reported revenues by 10 percent almost every month before the system was even in place, assuming that it was better to play by the rules and stop hiding revenue before it was too late and harsh penalties were applied.

5.5   BAZARS

In a lot of developing countries, a substantial part of small commerce is conducted in bazars.[5] Bazars are open-air market places where thousands of traders convene and set up tables or stalls to sell everything from food and home appliances to furniture and car parts. Georgia is no exception. The problem is that these transactions are conducted without any registration of traders or taxation of sales. This is why bazars account for a substantial share of the shadow economy. As part of its effort to clean up the economy, the Georgian government attempted to regulate bazars, and collect taxes from traders, as early as 2006. It was a well-intentioned move, but it came too early. Thousands of traders gathered to protest in front of the government building, saying that they shouldn't pay taxes when many other, much wealthier people did not. In many other such cases, the government proceeded with its reforms anyway. But in this case, the protesters were right. A substantial part of Georgia's economy, including many big players, had not come clean at the time, while the protesters were low-income merchants serving poor people. The bazars were the only places where they could conduct their modest business. The reform was suspended – a major blow to tax reform at the time.

In 2011, the government launched a second attempt to regulate bazars. A special, simplified tax was introduced for small traders. They did not have to pay VAT, calculate their profit, or pay an income tax. All they had to do was pay 4 percent on their total revenue. In conjunction with this move, the government reached out to those who owned the land on which the bazars were held. Since they collected rent from all traders, they were the people who knew the traders' revenues best. Land owners agreed to act as tax agents and collect taxes on behalf of the government. To make the collection process easier and more transparent, the government tried to take cash out of the equation. The proposed concept was modeled on supermarkets. The plan was to give new, big plots of land to landowners, obliging them to develop these plots and build clean, comfortable facilities. A central storage unit was to be constructed, and the plot would have to be accessed through a gated entry and exit point. Customers would not pay merchants in cash, but receive tickets for each transaction and pay for all purchased goods at the exit. That way, it would be much easier to create transparency about each trader's revenues. At the end of each day, traders would present their slips to the central cashier and receive cash for their sales, less the rent and the flat 4 percent tax. Unfortunately, the concept was never fully implemented. Nevertheless, it is a promising approach that could help other countries fight the shadow economy.

5.6 THE ESTONIAN MODEL

In Estonia, undistributed profit is not taxed. In other words, the tax on profits is only collected when profit is paid out to the owner, or owners, of a business as a dividend. If the profit is re-invested in the business, it is not taxed at all. This approach has come to be known as the Estonian model.[6] It has two major advantages:

1. *Investment incentive.* Because re-invested profit is not taxed, the model creates additional economic activity, development, and employment.
2. *Simplification.* Calculating profit tax is the number one source of disputes between private enterprises and the tax department. Since only dividends are taxed, profit does not have to be calculated in the first place. All regulation for tax purposes governing deferment of losses, depreciation, amortization, and transfer pricing between related companies within the country can be abolished. The resulting tax code is very simple and leaves little room for interpretation and corruption.

However, the Estonian model also has two minor drawbacks:

1. *Need for new regulation.* New rules have to be introduced to clarify which expenses qualify as investments. This is to prevent business owners from evading taxation by using corporate funds for personal expenses, such as cars, houses, or vacations, and labeling these expenses as investments, a maneuver that lets them extract money without paying the dividend tax. While rules to prevent this kind of fraud are much simpler than those governing the calculation of profits, it still requires an extra legislative effort initially.
2. *Dip in tax revenue.* When introduced, the Estonian model causes a temporary decrease in tax revenue. This is because business owners are usually excited about any new opportunity to save taxes and stop paying out dividends. But this effect quickly wears off. Sooner or later, business owners want to enjoy their profits, resume dividend payments, and start paying taxes again.

In Estonia, the dip in tax revenue leveled off after two years and was fully compensated for by an increase in later years. The Georgian government considered introducing the Estonian model but found that proceeds from the tax on profits represented too high a share of total tax revenue (more than 12 percent) at the time, and that there were no financial resources to compensate for the losses during the first few years. At the time of writing, Georgia is making a new effort to introduce the Estonian model, according to press reports: "The government [...] is keen to introduce the Estonian tax model, by which private companies will be exempt from profit tax if they re-invest their profit back into their businesses."[7] The introduction was approved by the parliament on May 13, 2016, and it will take effect in January 2017.[8] This development should definitely trigger higher economic activity in 2017.

5.7   CUSTOMS REFORM

Much like the tax code, customs regulations were also radically simplified to minimize ambiguity and prevent corruption. But unlike the police department (see chapter on "Fighting Corruption"), the customs department was not reformed overnight. Rather, changes were introduced step by step. Arguing that customs officers need specific knowledge, the administration initially let many old officers keep their jobs and work alongside the new recruits. In reality, the "old guard" realized that the new hires were there to replace them. In an act of self-preservation, they got their new colleagues implicated in their corrupt schemes. This made cleaning up the customs department one of the most difficult, and most time-consuming, part of the fight against corruption in Georgia. The reform wasn't complete until 2011, when most of the old employees had finally been let go and new special customs zones (see later in the chapter) had been created.

The overarching objective of the customs reform was twofold: simplify procedures for the private sector and decrease corruption by ramping up monitoring mechanisms. Key elements of the simplification included:

- The number of customs duties was reduced from 16 to 3 (with rates of 0, 5, and 12 percent). Over 80 percent of all imported goods were cleared at a rate of 0 percent. This made Georgia one of the most open economies in the region. The new customs code is the least protectionist, and most simple, such system in the world.
- All customs services were made part of a one-stop clearance process. Previously, anyone crossing the Georgian border had to go through

many different check points and get stamps and seals of approval from representatives of as many as half a dozen different government agencies: phytosanitary services overseen by the Ministry of Agriculture (animal and plant disease control), the Department of Cultural Heritage overseen by the Ministry of Culture, the border police overseen by the Ministry of the Interior, the customs department overseen by the revenue service, and so on. The change was as radical as it was simple. In future, all agencies – except for the border police – would be represented by the customs department. If there were any questions regarding the regulation governing particular products, the customs officer was to contact the relevant government agency and clear the goods on its behalf.

- A "golden list" containing the most customs-compliant importers and exporters was compiled. Companies that had a track record of clean books, honest customs declarations, and reliable payments were allowed to take imported goods directly to their warehouses through a special (so called "green") customs corridor. Additionally, they were allowed to pay customs duties with a 30-day delay. These privileges motivated other companies to follow suit, and become more compliant, to be included in the list.

- To support the hub economy concept (see Chap. 4, Creating a Business-Friendly Climate), special customs regulations were introduced, allowing goods to be stored in designated customs-free zones. Customs clearance was due only once the stored goods were sold, an approach that resembles the free port concept that was in effect in Hamburg, Germany, for more than a century. In Georgia, special customs zones were, and still are, widely used by car traders. They import cars to Georgia's special customs zones and only pay customs clearance duties when the cars are sold, often to buyers from other countries in the region. Before long, the designated special customs zones became the places where imported cars are mainly traded. As a result, Georgia has become the biggest car-trading hub in the region, leading to the creation of about 20,000 new jobs.

Additionally, the customs code itself was clarified to eliminate ambiguity; see Chap. 2, Fighting Corruption, for details. These and other simplifications made the clearance process much more business-friendly and greatly improved customs compliance. However, the simplifications were not sufficient to eradicate corruption at Georgia's borders completely. This is why additional monitoring measures were introduced:

- *Hardware.* The government invested in technology to facilitate checks and improve surveillance in customs areas. Scanners and cameras were hot-linked to the surveillance center at the Ministry of Finance. This was to prevent customs officers from manipulating the data feed. Cameras covered all areas of the customs clearance process, from the border crossing itself to the areas in which vehicles and cargo were inspected. The live feed was transmitted directly to the surveillance center, and any misconduct was punished without pardon or exception.
- *Software.* The ASYCUDA[9] software system, developed by the United Nations and widely used by customs authorities worldwide, was introduced in Georgia. It is based on four tiers of scrutiny that correspond to color-coded customs gates: green, blue, yellow, and red. Green stands for free passage without any check, while red stands for a detailed check on the spot. Every importer has to pass one of these gates. The color is assigned by an automated risk assessment system. This module is the most important part of the new system; the risk assessment module automatically assigns a given batch of goods to one of the four color-coded gates. Customs officers are not allowed to interfere with the assignment, which is made based on historical data about a given company, a given type of product, and a given country of origin. The automation prevents customs officials from abusing their position of power and granting preferential treatment to importers in exchange for bribes. *Ad hoc* checks of vehicles or cargo are only permissible under exceptional circumstances and require approval by a supervisor.

The reforms described previously improved the performance of the customs department substantially. The biggest leap came in 2011, when the special customs zones were built. All the previously described policies were in effect in these zones, and the customs department introduced some additional innovations to make the clearance process even more transparent and business friendly:

- All vehicles that crossed the border and carried goods for import were directed to the closest special customs zone.

- If the clearance process was not completed within 30 minutes, a supervisor would get involved. If the delay was the fault of a customs officer, that officer would be let go. If the delay was due to ambiguous regulations, these regulations would promptly be clarified.
- Brokers were eliminated and all procedures, including the completion of customs forms, were taken over by representatives of the revenue service.

Getting rid of brokers turned out to be the biggest challenge. It is a service that exists in many countries. The broker helps importers deal with the customs department and fill out special customs clearance forms. Filling out these forms was, in fact, a big hurdle for importers in Georgia. They were very complicated and required knowledge of special product codes with which most ordinary business people were unfamiliar. Most brokers were former customs officials with close relations to active members of the customs department. Because of these ties, brokers were able not only to help importers with their forms, but also to charge special fees for preferential treatment. Although it was hard to prove, the general assumption was that brokers passed on a part of the fees they charged to active customs officials. In any case, eliminating these intermediaries made the customs clearance process much more transparent. Employees of the revenue service took the place of brokers and helped importers fill out the required forms. According to independent research, customer satisfaction increased immensely, and Transparency International confirmed that customs-related corruption was reduced. Here is a verbatim statement by an importer: "Three years ago, to import anything, you had to visit ten rooms and pay someone extra money in each room for getting all your papers in order. It created a whole chain of corruption and delay that involved everybody. Today it's much easier. It's very organized there now. There's one room now, and we know in advance how much we'll have to pay."[10]

NOTES

1. http://www.transparency.org/research/gcb/overview (retrieved in May 2016).
2. E-filing is defined as "the process of using a computer program to transmit information electronically to another party." (http://www.businessdiction ary.com/definition/e-file.html#ixzz49eyuFP7x; retrieved in May 2016).

3. Out of the ten, four were the "Big Four" – international players and six were local companies.
4. In the private sector, a mystery shopper is a person "hired by a market research firm or a manufacturer to visit retail stores, posing as a casual shopper to collect information about the stores' display, prices, and quality of their sales staff." (http://www.businessdictionary.com/definition/mys tery-shopper.html#ixzz49f3rhd00; retrieved in May 2016).
5. Bazar, sometimes also translated as bazaar, is the Persian word for market.
6. http://www.amcham.ge/diary/rtable_2016-03-09/estonian-model.pdf (retrieved in May 2016).
7. http://mondediplo.com/blogs/georgia-neoliberalism-and-industrial-pol icy (retrieved in May 2016).
8. http://www.messenger.com.ge/issues/3629_may_17_2016/3629_econ_ one.html (retrieved in May 2016).
9. ASYCUDA stands for Automated System for Customs Data (https://www. asycuda.org/; retrieved in May 2016).
10. Stephen F. Jones, The Making of Modern Georgia, Routledge, London/ New York 2014 (p. 108); http://pdf.usaid.gov/pdf_docs/Pdacn591.pdf (retrieved in May 2016) (Jones 2014).

CHAPTER 6

Privatizing State-Owned Enterprises

Abstract This chapter describes the formulas for privatization that were used to privatize almost all state-owned assets in Georgia between 2004 and 2011, including its ports, airports, water utilities, and power grid. To improve service levels and ensure long-term economic feasibility for investors, the government followed a best-practice process, comprising five steps – from replacing top managers and laying down the regulatory framework for the future private companies to screening and selecting bidders. The chapter also explains why Georgia's railway and its oil and gas corporation were exempt from full privatization. It concludes with a discussion of alternatives to outright privatization, such as issuing Eurobonds and establishing public-private partnership funds, which combine the benefits of competitive pressure on public enterprises with governmental control.

Keywords Railway · State-owned-enterprises · London stock exchange (LSE) · IPO · Partnership fund (PF) · Public Private Partnership (PPP)

Between 2004 and 2011, Georgia privatized almost all state-owned assets, including its ports, airports, water utilities, and power grid. To improve service levels, protect the long-term interests of the state, and

© The Author(s) 2017
N. Gilauri, *Practical Economics*,
DOI 10.1007/978-3-319-45769-7_6

ensure sufficiently attractive returns for investors, the government followed a five-step process:

1. *Step one* was to replace top management with new or interim managers, since incumbent directors showed little interest in successful privatization.
2. *Step two* was to restructure state-owned enterprises, in particular to lay off those employees who had been hired for the wrong reasons. This step was both painful and unpopular, but inevitable, since even the smallest inefficiency would have increased the bargaining power of potential investors.
3. *Step three* was to lay down the regulatory framework for the future private companies, e.g., their suppliers, customers, and mid-term obligations.
4. *Step four* was to draft tender documents and privatization agreements.
5. *Step five* was to screen and select bidders in an open auction.

Only Georgia's railway and its oil and gas corporation were exempt from privatization for geopolitical reasons. These assets remain under public control, but the government has taken innovative steps to improve their performance.

6.1   THE CHALLENGE

State-owned enterprises (SOEs) everywhere are a hotbed for inefficiency, and Georgia was no exception. In the early 2000s, corruption was the norm at its SOEs. Politicians treated SOEs as their personal cash cows, and most decisions were driven by greed, rather than by an interest to promote the greater good of the country as a whole. For example, members of government routinely appointed people to leadership positions at SOEs in return for handouts or other favors. This is what it's like in many other countries, be they developed or developing, even today. Unless the government takes special precautions, SOEs invariably veer toward inefficiency and corruption. The root cause of this tendency is the fact that the state, as the owner, has little inherent interest in maximizing the profit of an SOE. There are plenty of other sources of budgetary income, such as taxes and customs, and the resources of SOEs can be used in many ways other than to maximize net profit: to finance politically sensitive projects and hide them from parliamentary review, to secure the favor of voters prior to an election, or simply to find employment for friends and family. That's what things were like in Georgia before 2004.

Whenever calls for privatization arise, politicians routinely deploy heavy rhetorical artillery: the state should hold on to its assets and keep strategic companies under public control. Foreign companies should not be allowed to take over, or even manage, any "national treasures." Such populist appeals to pride and nationalism resonate well with many people, especially in small developing countries. In reality, most politicians who make this sort of declaration are only trying to protect their jobs or their illicit income.

So how should utility, energy, and transport be managed in a modern democracy? Is privatization the only option to prevent corruption and increase efficiency? Are certain types of state-owned companies better suited to privatization than others? Which assets, if any, should be exempt from privatization?

The lesson we learned in Georgia, and elsewhere, is that privatization is a double-edged sword. If you handle it well, it is a powerful tool that will make the state stronger and bring benefit to the population. If, however, it is handled unprofessionally, let alone in a corrupt manner, it will inflict harm on the state and bring disadvantage to its citizens. In any case, state-owned enterprises should be restructured prior to privatization, and proper regulation should be put in place to make sure future owners of SOEs don't exploit their position as *de facto* monopolists at the expense of the public. As a general rule, at least two investors should be shortlisted for any privatization effort to ensure some measure of competition. SOEs from other countries should not normally be admitted as investors to take over an SOE. One SOE buying up another SOE doesn't really qualify as privatization, and it doesn't bring the full benefit from the perspective of the state. Even if future losses will be absorbed by another government, chances are that the new company will be no more efficient than its predecessor. Finally, governments should not hesitate to hire reputable consulting companies to help with the legal, financial, and transactional aspects of the privatization process, or even have contractors manage SOEs for a limited transitional period prior to privatization. All potential investors will be working with the best experts in their fields, and the least a responsible government can do is make sure it is on an equal footing with bidders in this respect. Negotiating a well-structured, profitable deal is no small matter. It goes beyond the expertise of even the finest public servants, which is why the fees of experts will easily pay for themselves.

In Georgia, we followed a five-step privatization process, and it served us well. I recommend that other countries take inspiration from it and adapt it to their needs.

6.2   THE FIVE-STEP PROCESS

Step 1 is to replace the CEO and directors of the company. Nobody likes to kill their darlings, and if you have managed a company for years, or even decades, that company inevitably will have become your darling. You will feel that you have given it your all, and that your team has done the best it could – the best, in fact, anybody could have done under the circumstances. From the perspective of a veteran, bringing in new managers will look like a waste of resources. Nine out of ten times, an incumbent CEO will not support the privatization process. Leaving an SOE's top team in place prior to privatization is the biggest mistake governments can make. The old guard will often not disclose relevant information to potential investors they don't approve of, at least not fully and truthfully, and they will impair the impact of privatization by striking shady deals with the future owners of the SOE to keep their jobs. The mission of an incoming CEO and top team should be very clear: ensure successful privatization, period. Typically, this is a temporary rather than a permanent assignment, and the government should be clear about this from the start. The objective for the new management is to restructure the company and sell it. Ideally, remuneration is tied to the total value created through the privatization contract, including the price of the sale and any investment obligations imposed on the new owner.

Step 2 is to restructure the company. Almost all SOEs are inefficient in one way or another. Common issues include:

- Employees hired solely as a favor to politicians
- Managers promoted to positions of leadership based on tenure or political affiliation, rather than qualification or performance
- Onerous contracts causing the SOE incessant losses

To fix these issues, you need political consensus that the company is to be privatized, and that the government should take the appropriate measures to find a high-caliber investor, get the best possible price, and secure the commitment of the prospective new owner to invest in the company in future. To achieve these objectives, the company must be as lean and efficient as possible *prior* to privatization – lay off employees who are not needed, replace managers who are not qualified for their positions, and re-negotiate or terminate unfavorable contracts. It is a common, but costly, mistake to leave these issues to the new owners. The fact is that every little inefficiency of an SOE gives undue bargaining power to potential investors during negotiations and will decrease the total value of the privatization contract.

Step 3 is to set up a proper regulatory framework. It should cover the following questions: Are the processes required to ensure proper checks and balances already in place? Or will it be very difficult for the government to understand what is going on in the sector in question after privatization? Specifically, is a proper reporting requirement in place to keep the government in the loop? What is the structure of the tariff system? Is it sufficiently attractive to attract reputable companies as investors and ensure they resist the temptation of making money on the side? Is there any danger of the new owner exploiting the mono-polistic position of the company? If yes, which precautions are required to minimize the risk of the new owner besting the state or its custo-mers? Rules and regulations for the sector in question must be clear and transparent to all parties to enable them to take fact-based, well-informed decisions.

Step 4 is to prepare the tender documents and draft the actual privatiza-tion agreement, ideally with the help of well-established international consultants. The contract should not only specify the terms and condi-tions of the deal itself, but also spell out the investment obligations of the future owner for the next five to seven years. The deal should be structured in a way that balances multiple objectives:

- Provide an attractive investment opportunity for the bidder
- Attract investment to the company and make it more efficient
- Help the rest of the economy become more competitive
- Secure better service in the sector in question
- Maximize total long-term value creation for the state

Step 5 is the actual selection process. This should start with a roadshow and advertisements as required to attract the best players in the sector or industry in question. An open auction should be held with the most suitable bidders. For details on auctions, also see the chapter on Fighting Corruption.

Typically, the right to participate in the first round of negotiations will go to the bidder offering the highest price. The highest sale price, however, will not always be the best deal. From the perspective of the state, value creation can take many different shapes. More efficient operations, better management, transfer of know-how, and future investment obligations can easily compensate for a slightly lower sale price. In any case, the contract should protect the long-term interests of the state and allow the investor to make a good, clean profit in the medium term. That is why it is very important to define and communicate the selection criteria and their weighting upfront: Will the final decision be taken based on price alone? Will obligations regarding future investments play a role? What about management experience and technical expertise? Personally, I have found that it is best to use only criteria that can be quantified in the last tender and to create a clear-cut formula as to how they will factor in the decision. Qualitative criteria, such as an experienced management team, should only be used in the initial screening stage. In other words, bidders who do not fulfill these criteria should not even be admitted to the final round. And once a bidder is admitted to the final round, qualitative criteria should not be applied again, assuming that all participants who have made it this far satisfy the government's qualitative requirements.

Regarding the final round itself, it is crucial to create a formula that all parties understand. This is exactly what we did when we put one of the utilities in Georgia out for tender. From the perspective of the government, it was crucial for the tariffs to stay as low as possible for as long as possible, and we made this clear to all potential investors. We also defined the investments the future owner of the utility would have to make over the course of the coming years. Based on these preconditions, we asked potential investors to submit proposals specifying tariff levels for the next seven years and the price they were willing to pay. The formula we would apply to select the winning proposal was predefined and clearly communicated to bidders: a specific weight was given to the tariff for every year, and these weights added up to account for 50 percent of the decision. The remaining 50 percent weight was attached to the price the bidder was willing to pay. Thanks to the transparent approach, this turned out to be one of the most efficient tenders we ever conducted.

6.3 THE OUTCOME IN GEORGIA

Between 2004 and 2011, almost all state-owned assets in Georgia were successfully privatized based on the five-step process outlined previously. Examples include ports and airports, electricity and gas distribution companies, hydroelectric power plants, and water utility companies. These efforts were successful in several respects:

- Investors fulfilled the obligations imposed under the respective privatization contracts. Specifically, they invested substantial amounts of capital and transformed formerly troubled SOEs into financially sound private companies.
- The new companies grew in terms of efficiency and effectiveness.
- Consumers and corporate customers were happy with how the new companies performed and the services they provided.
- Investors were happy. They made sizable upfront investments, but now they are reaping the rewards in the form of substantial profits.

In 2005, for example, Tbilisi airport was privatized by way of a build-operate-transfer (BOT) contract with TAV, a Turkish company that also operates the airports of Istanbul in Turkey, Skopje in Macedonia, Zagreb in Croatia, and in many other cities in the region. In 2007, Tbilisi airport was thoroughly renovated and expanded, tripling its annual passenger capacity. Today, the airport connects Georgia to various international destinations such as Rome, Paris, Moscow, Istanbul, Dubai, Frankfurt and others. In contrast, privatization efforts were less successful in those cases in which a Georgian SOE was taken over by an SOE from another country. The investments the foreign SOEs made were usually both insufficient and inefficient. Generally, the new companies did not receive the attention and the support they would have required.

But the vast majority of privatization efforts was successful. Our experience shows that privatized companies are more efficient than SOEs, and that they contribute to economic growth within and beyond their industries, more so than SOEs. Because private companies are profit-oriented and cannot rely on state subsidies, they are forced to innovate more, to attract better personnel, to develop better know-how, to invest more in R&D, and to adopt superior management practices. And unlike most SOEs, they do not consume public funds. Instead, they contribute to the state's budget by paying taxes, and the proceeds of privatization itself can be invested by the government to develop new infrastructure. Generally, managers of privatized companies have a much bigger incentive to improve performance than the directors of SOEs, which is why all state-owned assets should be privatized – unless privatization brings undue geopolitical tension.

6.4   STRATEGIC ASSETS

Since the dawn of capitalism, politicians and economists have debated the limits of privatization. Are there any companies that a government should never sell because of strategic considerations? For example, will the privatization of electricity distribution, electricity transmission, or railway operations put the country at a disadvantage in times of geopolitical turmoil? The experience in Georgia shows that there are, in fact, such strategic assets, and that the government should not sell them, at least not without taking proper precautions to protect the interests of the state. However, our experience also shows that the nature of such strategic assets differs from country to country. What is more, we also found that there is an attractive middle ground between state ownership and blunt privatization, and that some strategic assets can be considered for partial privatization, provided the underlying contract is well designed and regulation is appropriate to protect the interests of the state. In a nutshell: you can sell anything, or almost anything, if the contract and the regulation are watertight.

Examples of privatizing these so-called strategic assets and due to prudent regulations being still under control even during most difficult geopolitical situation, include privatization of Telasi, Tbilisi's electricity distribution company, and the partial divestment (50 percent share) of the transmission line connecting the Georgian and Russian energy grids. In both cases, although the investors were state-owned or state-controlled Russian companies, neither of these entities were used against Georgia's interests during the Russian invasion. The regulation that was put in place was well crafted and very straight forward and the management of the companies knew very well that in case it acted against the national interests of the government they would have been taken over (managerially not ownership wise) by the regulator. During the war, these companies followed closely instructions from the central dispatcher, and energy supply was neither interrupted nor impaired at any point. Thanks to good regulation, strategic assets remained under the government's control during this sensitive period.

Surely, experts in most countries would classify electricity distribution and the high-voltage power grid as highly sensitive and potentially vulnerable parts of a state's technical infrastructure. But if even these assets can be in the hands of a hostile foreign power during a war without harm coming to the country, which other assets, if any, should the government not privatize for strategic reasons? In Georgia's case, it was the Georgian Railway (GR) and the Georgian Oil and Gas Corporation (GOGC).

Because of tense political relations between two of Georgia's neighbors, Azerbaijan and Armenia, privatizing the GR and the GOGC could have turned into a geopolitical conflict, a conflict that would have been disastrous for the whole region and for Georgia itself. This is because almost all of Armenia's imports use the GR, and almost 100 percent of Armenia's gas consumption goes through the GOGC. Everybody agreed that political stability was much more important than any commercial benefit that might come from the privatization of these assets. The Georgian government decided to hold on to the GR and the GOGC, lest they be used as geopolitical weapons by an investor, a foreign power, or any other party.

In these cases, privatization was not an option. However, we still wanted to improve efficiency and introduce a certain performance culture at the GR and the GOGC. The solution we found was to have these companies issue corporate Eurobonds at the London Stock Exchange. The idea was to measure the performance of the top team, and reward it with bonuses, based on the difference between sovereign Eurobonds (issued by Georgia's national government) and corporate Eurobonds (issued by GR and the GOGC).[1] In effect, we had the world's financial markets assess the performance of the respective management teams for us. High demand, and the resulting high valuation, of GR and GOGC bonds would signify that investors believed in the leadership teams and did not see major risks regarding the future performance of these companies. This step motivated the managers at GR and the GOGC to be transparent, seek close relations with investors, and to adopt best management practices. As a side effect – managers of these companies acted as best salespersons of the country itself – as most questions from investors were about the country's economic situation. All of this helped to advance the performance not only of these companies but also of Georgia's economy as a whole, and I believe that other developing countries would benefit in similar ways.

As mentioned previously – privatization can go wrong and hurt a country's economy for long term. In the Ukraine, for example, the privatization of state assets went wrong in a big way in the 1990s. It resulted in a situation in which a handful of oligarchs control most of these assets, a major obstacle to the country's growth. The oligarchs in Ukraine, in many cases, have their own political parties, control part of the media and control different parts of the government. They are primarily motivated by the desire to defend/increase their wealth and fortify their political positions, not by any great urge to advance the prosperity of the country as a whole. Their interests do not coincide with the interests of the country and any positive initiative by one is accepted by others as a potential threat and is blocked.

In the autumn of 2015, I was invited to Kiev to present Georgian economic reforms to the Ukrainian government. After presenting the Georgian story to all stakeholders (members of government and IFIs, representatives of private sector and NGOs) I met with a Ukrainian minister of economy. As a way out of the predicament, I offered him an out-of-box solution that may have changed the country and create a stepping stone for the turnaround path of Ukrainian economy. The idea was to adopt a legislation that would oblige the oligarchs within specific a timeframe to take their companies to international financial markets (e.g., London Stock Exchange) to IPO (formula for privatization – Initial Public Offering). This may have been very much accepted by all oligarchs as all of them, being in the same situation, would have been calm that nobody is taking their assets from them (but they are maximizing their wealth on the international financial markets) and would force them to act in the best interests of the country – their successful IPOs and thus their wealth would depend on how well country is performing. On top, they would be forced to attract best managers with international experience in their companies, clean up the most important assets, and start paying taxes fully. The minister loved the idea. He shook my hand and said that he would do his best to take the proposal to the president and that he would come back to me. He never did. The government of the Ukraine, including the minister of economy, has since been succeeded by a new administration. It still remains to be seen if the new government will be up to thinking out of the box and adopt this or a similar regulation. Using existing experiences only may not be the best solution for particular problems. Innovative approaches to new problems are required in cases and the Ukrainian case, I believe, is one of them.

6.5   PARTNERSHIP FUNDS

Another tool to improve the performance of SOEs without privatizing them is to set up public-private partnership funds. The Georgian government established such a partnership fund in 2010, set up as a holding entity that holds shares of large SOEs and uses dividend income, privatization proceeds, or bond proceeds to develop new infrastructure in cooperation with the private sector. The main objective was to assist international investors with the financing of large-scale infrastructure projects. Because of the relatively small size of Georgia's economy at the time, it was difficult to convince investors to shoulder the full risk of major infrastructure investments without public co-financing or state guarantees. Promising projects were stalled because investors felt the investment was too large relative to the size of the country's economy. These projects promised robust returns on investment, but they required investments exceeding 6 percent of Georgia's GDP, and investors would only consider these projects if the state would chip in with co-financing or back them up with guarantees.

The government, however, was unwilling to give outright guarantees. This was because the country had had negative experiences with such guarantees in the past. They had mostly been used to fill the coffers of corrupt individuals rather than to help develop the country's economy. So the partnership fund (PF) was created. Its objective was to help the private sector with major investments in infrastructure that would benefit the country as a whole without having to grant governmental guarantees. The PF held shares of all major SOEs – such as GR, GOGC, and GSE[2] – and was the financial beneficiary of these companies, but the PF was not to be involved in the day-to-day management of these SOEs. The primary role of the PF was to set dividend policies for these companies in cooperation with the Ministry of Finance and other relevant ministries. Additionally, the PF would invest in large-scale infrastructure projects in cooperation with the private sector.

Initially, it was anything but trivial to find the golden middle ground between a hands-off investment approach and a hands-on management approach. The private sector was concerned that the PF would act as their competitor. Which sectors would it get involved in? What, exactly, would its goal be? Turn a profit for the government? Create jobs? Bring consumer prices down? Would the PF have privileged access to foreign direct investment in a particular sector at the expense of private companies? How would the fund choose its partners – based on experience, on co-financing, or in exchange for bribes? All of these concerns brought uncertainty to the economy, at least initially. Yet we believed that it was worth the effort to hang in and resolve these issues. The PF was, quite simply, the only way to get big things built in a small economy like Georgia, where the construction of a single large Hydro Power Plant (HPP) would require an investment in the magnitude of 10 percent of the country's GDP.

To address the concerns of the private sector and hedge the risk of the investment, Georgia's PF was given very limited powers. The areas and specific projects in which the PF would invest were specified in advance. The fund was only to invest in projects of a certain size, and its co-financing capacity was restricted to a maximum of 49 percent of equity. Also, the fund was obliged to sell its share in any project within four to five years to the private partner company or another investor. Additionally, a special supervisory board was established. It consisted of members of the government and representatives of the private sector, mainly of the banking sector. This was to prevent the PF from competing with private banks for suitable projects and from taking business away from them.

Unfortunately, the PF did not consult the board as actively as the government had originally envisaged. This created considerable unrest among private sector players. These drawbacks do not, however, discredit the concept of a state-owned financial vehicle tasked with helping private investors finance large infrastructure projects in developing countries. They merely illustrate that any such vehicle requires a clear definition of its role and duties by legislation, as well as meticulous management and oversight, to make sure it benefits both the public and the private sector.

Notes

1. http://www.investopedia.com/terms/s/sovereignbond.asp; http://www.investopedia.com/terms/c/corporatebond.asp (retrieved in May 2016).
2. Georgian Railway, Georgian Oil and Gas Corporation, and Georgian State Electrosystem.

CHAPTER 7

Reforming the Energy Sector

Abstract This chapter describes how Georgia modernized its energy sector. When Nika Gilauri took office as minister of energy in 2004, blackouts were the norm, power was supplied to customers only for a few hours a day, and only about 30 percent of the power used was actually paid for. The Ministry of Energy itself suffered frequent power outages. The situation was further aggravated by seasonal effects. In Georgia, where hydroelectric power is the primary source of energy, generation peaks in summer, but consumption peaks in the cold winters. As a result, Georgia has long depended on seasonal energy imports and was deep in debt with all neighboring countries. This chapter tells the story of how the government turned things around through decisive industry restructuring. By 2006, the country had 24-hour energy supply even in remote areas, and the payment rate had reached 96 percent. And one year later, in 2007, Georgia has turned into net electricity exporter.

Keywords Blackouts · Tariff · Enguri · UDC · Single-buyer · GSE

7.1 Georgia's Energy Sector in 2004

The reform of the energy sector was one of the most crucial, and most visible, reforms undertaken in Georgia between 2004 and 2007. It was vital for the economic development of the country. No business can prosper when electricity blackouts are the norm. What is more, this reform

© The Author(s) 2017
N. Gilauri, *Practical Economics*,
DOI 10.1007/978-3-319-45769-7_7

was also politically crucial for the success of the new government. The desolate state of the energy sector was one of the key drivers of dissatisfaction with the previous government. In fact, it was among the main reasons for the Rose Revolution, and everybody expected significant improvements.

In 2004, the Georgian energy sector was riddled with all sorts of issues – technical, economic, and political:

- *Technical.* The electricity grid was not equipped to operate independently. It had been designed during the Soviet era to operate within the much larger system spanning the Caucasus and southern Russia. And because maintenance had long been neglected, most transmission lines needed replacement. Operations depended on a handful of people who knew how to work the controls. Most of the distribution network lacked metering. There was no transparency about who was consuming how much energy. Hydropower and thermal power plants suffered from malfunction on a daily basis. Some of the largest hydroelectric power plants were in fact permanently out of order. In the winter, electricity was supplied to customers only for two to three hours per day. In some regions, supply was as low as two to three hours per week. Customers had long given up hopes of 24-hour supply. Rather, they demanded to be notified in advance of when to expect the two to three hours of supply they had grown accustomed to. The Ministry of Energy itself had no electricity.
- *Economic.* The tariff system was inappropriate. Even if all fees had been collected, the electricity sector would still have been losing money. But in fact, the collection rate was below 30 percent, and as low as 10 percent in some cases. There were no funds to maintain the system or even pay salaries. The staff of most energy sector companies had not been paid for 20–24 months. As a consequence, there were strikes at hydroelectric power plants and dispatch centers almost every week. Worst of all, the limited proceeds of the energy sector were used to subsidize the rest of the economy. Because of its structure, size, and corrupt practices, the energy sector was not only the main source of income for high-level public officials (especially in regions outside of the capital Tbilisi), but it was also one of the main sources of subsidies for other sectors, many of which were based on corrupt deals brokered by top decision makers. For example, one of the largest consumers of electrical power, a ferroalloy plant, did not

pay for energy at all because it was under the protection of the president Shevardnadze's family members. Some villages in one of the regions did not pay for gas because they were very active politically. Other villages simply diverted gas from pipelines that passed through their territory illegally.

- *Political.* In 2003, energy was one of the most corrupt sectors in Georgia. As the only industry that generated any cash at a regional level, it was the main source of illegal income for regional government representatives. Many criminals were making money in the sector. Whatever money was collected by the distribution companies was not re-invested but pocketed by the managers of the distribution companies who paid off both government officials (to avoid prosecution) and criminals (to prevent attacks). On a more mundane level, theft of gas pipes was a frequent occurrence. The single largest producer of electricity (Enguri, Vardnili Cascade power plants) was located in a territory that was not controlled by the government of Georgia, in a Russian occupied region of Abkhazia, although the dam was on controlled territory. As a result, there was next to no accountability and very limited control. On a national level, the energy sector had debts with all of Georgia's neighboring countries, both for electricity and gas delivery.

The energy sector had been broken down into many different companies and entities. As a result, nobody was responsible for anything. Decentralization may work well for countries in which there are no energy problems, and where everything is running smoothly, such as the United States or many Western European countries. But in developing countries with energy problems, decentralization makes things worse. Without central accountability and oversight, officials blame each other for blackouts and other issues. In Georgia, distribution companies were blaming the transmission company for the blackouts. The transmission company was blaming dispatch, and dispatch was blaming the generation companies. Generation companies were blaming GWEM (the Georgian Wholesale Electricity Market operator), and everybody was blaming the Ministry of Energy and the independent regulator (GNERC). In turn, the central institutions blamed every company and agency further down the chain. Paradoxically, they all had a valid point.

Two years later, Georgia had 24-hour electricity supply, except for a few days after Russia blew up two gas pipelines and one high-voltage line simultaneously. The collection rate went from 30 percent in 2004 to 91 percent in 2007 (including commercial losses) – one of the fastest jumps ever seen in this figure globally. By 2007, Georgia was a net electricity exporter. Let's look at how Georgia made it happen. While some solutions were specific to Georgia, others will be instructive to many countries facing energy problems, be they small or big, developed, or developing.

7.2   TEMPORARY CENTRALIZATION OF COMMAND FOR IMPROVED ACCOUNTABILITY

Before the reforms, different agencies were responsible for different decisions. Long-term policy was formulated by the Ministry of Energy. The annual electricity balance was approved by GWEM (the Georgian Wholesale Electricity Market operator). The tariff scheme and regulatory rules were approved by an independent regulator (GNERC). New regulation gave all powers, except for tariff approval, to the Ministry of Energy. Even tariffs were negotiated with companies on a case-by-case basis by the ministry, and only final legal approval was in the hands of the GNERC. Even though the Ministry of Economy formally owned the energy companies, the Ministry of Energy appointed their directors. In effect, all decision-making power started to be concentrated in one institution. This also meant that the ministry was fully responsible for what happened in the sector. It could not blame anybody else for poor performance. This was the key to the success of the reforms. Once the crisis was contained, the government started to decentralize the sector again step by step.

7.3   CHANGE OF STAFF AND MANAGEMENT CONTRACTS TO END CORRUPTION

At almost every energy company and every state agency, new management was put in place. Previously, salaries of civil servants had been so low that nobody could survive on them alone. Everybody was making money on the side. To put an end to these practices, new staff and new management were brought in from outside of the energy sector, and young low-level employees were promoted. In some cases, international companies were contracted to manage selected state-owned energy companies. This brought an influx of modern management practices and technical know-how. In Georgia, the presence of expatriates in the management of energy distribution companies was an important cata-lyst that made it easier to justify non-paying customers having their power supply disconnected. Somebody needed to take the blame for these tough decisions, and the expat managers served as scapegoats in the public eye.

7.4   COMMUNAL METERING TO DRIVE UP COLLECTION RATES

Low collection was the root of most evil in the energy sector. Because only about one-third of all power provided to customers was paid for, the sector lost money on every kWh sold. The payments simply did not cover the cost of production. Effectively, there was a negative incentive to produce any power at all. This is why the Ministry of Energy and the distribution companies focused their efforts on collection. Key measures included:

- *Legal changes*, which were introduced to make the theft of electricity, and tampering with meters, punishable by law.
- *Communal meters*, which were installed in all regions, as well as in many districts of large cities. Each communal meter covered 30–60 households. Payments were due based on the measurement of the communal meter. The distribution company disregarded individual meters, many of which had previously been manipulated or bypassed with so-called "fish hooks." If the distribution company did not receive full payment for energy supplied according to the communal meter, the whole community was disconnected. As soon as whole villages or communities were obliged to pay based on a communal meter, neighbors started keeping an eye out for "fish hooks" and disconnecting each other's illegal power lines. Initially, there was some unrest, but the political message was very clear: put up with communal metering or get by without electricity. Communities that paid were rewarded with 24-hour supply of electricity. This was to show other communities that those who paid did not just get elec-tricity for a few hours a day but around the clock. Local police chiefs who took the side of violators were fired. The policy became very well known in a short period of time, and protests against communal metering eventually calmed down. The next step was the rehabilita-tion of local distribution networks. Closed lines and new individual meters were installed.

- *Non-paying customers were disconnected.* Previously, distribution companies had not been able to disconnect their largest customers, such as major factories and transport companies. These had been identified as direct customers and were supplied directly by the GWEM (the Georgian Wholesale Electricity Market operator). Companies with close ties to the previous president's family or the government never paid their electricity bills, but nobody dared to disconnect them. They were untouchable. Hospitals did not pay their bills either. They blackmailed the energy sector, saying that if they were disconnected people might die. In fact, many hospitals were running profitable side businesses selling energy to local bakeries, restaurants, bars, and cafés through illegal lines. The new government put an end to these practices. Everybody had to pay their electricity bill in full. As Minister of Energy, I personally disconnected non-compliant hospitals to send a message that exceptions would no longer be tolerated. Specifically, all government agencies – army bases, prisons, water supply utilities – were obliged to pay their electricity bills in full. How can you expect the private sector to pay if the public sector doesn't? Going forward, every minister would have to budget for electricity payments, something that was unheard of until 2004.
- *Corrupt private distribution companies were banned.* In the early 2000s, corrupt officials had effectively privatized service to well-paying customers. These blackmailed the most profitable customers to switch from Georgia's main distribution company, UDC, to newly formed private distribution companies (DisCos). The owners of these DisCos, who usually were also managers or board members at state-owned distribution companies, would deliberately disconnect some parts of large cities and leave only DisCo customers with power. This was to demonstrate that switching to a DisCo would guarantee them better service, although even the customers of DisCos did not get 24-hour supply, simply because the system as a whole was in such poor repair. DisCos routinely cherry-picked the most solvent and most compliant customers, leaving public distributors with those who couldn't, or wouldn't, pay their bills. This privatization of profits pushed the whole sector toward bankruptcy and created additional sources of corruption. In 2004, the government decided to annul all private licenses and put all UDC assets

under the management of an independent international contractor. This change to the structure of the system was very difficult to push through, but it was one of the most important catalysts in Georgia's energy reform.

- *A simple incentive scheme was introduced.* Once the system of extortion by untouchable customers and embezzlement by corrupt officials was overcome, the Ministry of Energy proceeded to incentivize collection compliance. As part of the reforms, the UDC was split into 50 distribution regions. The grid was split between these regions in a way that made it next to impossible to cheat with regard to the electricity received by each region. From then on, every director of a region was assessed based only on the collection rate in that region. All other indicators were disregarded to keep the incentive scheme as simple as possible. Every month, the managers of the top-performing regions got a substantial bonus, and the managers of the lowest-performing regions were fired – every month, for nine months in a row. By the end of that period, the collection rate had tripled.

7.5   FROM SINGLE BUYER TO DEREGULATED STRUCTURE

Energy generation in Georgia is based on hydroelectric power in the summer, when there is typically an oversupply of energy, and gas-fired thermal power plants in the winter, when heating systems draw the most power. Gas needs to be imported, which means that energy production is five to six times as costly in the winter as it is in the summer. Before 2004, wintertime blackouts were the norm.

Prior to our reforms, not only distribution but also wholesale prices had been the same throughout the year, based on the actual average cost of generating energy in different seasons. This system was modeled on some European countries, but it proved inappropriate for Georgia. The plan was to have the Georgian Wholesale Electricity Market (GWEM) buy cheap hydroelectrically generated energy in the summer and sell it at prices above the cost of production. That way, the GWEM would build up funds in the summer, enabling it to sell thermal energy to customers below the high cost of production in the winter. The snag was that the build-up of funds in the summer never happened because of the low collection rate. So in the winter, the GWEM had to buy expensive energy from generators and sell it to customers cheaply. The power generated by hydroelectric power plants was insufficient to satisfy wintertime demand. To close the gap, Georgia had to import energy or switch on its gas-fired thermal power plants. But both options required full payment, often in advance because of the accumulated debt to providers in neighboring countries, for which there were no funds. In response to the inevitable shortages, the central dispatcher was ordered to disconnect customers, and the blaming game would start. Distribution companies blamed the GWEM for not having enough funds in the winter, the GWEM blamed distributors for not paying their bills during the summer, and everybody blamed the Ministry of Energy for the inappropriate pricing system. As a result, the energy sector ran into serious financial difficulties and required additional government subsidies every winter. In 2005, this system was abandoned. All distribution companies and large customers were given the freedom to purchase electricity directly from local energy providers or from importers – at prices covering the actual cost of generation at the time of consumption. Distribution companies were put in charge to prepare their individual electricity supply contracts independently. In parallel, wholesale price setting was de-regulated to reflect seasonal changes in supply and demand. Distribution companies finally had to pay higher prices in the winter, as they should have done from the beginning. The year the new system was introduced was the year Georgia put an end to the blackouts.

In addition, the Ministry of Energy negotiated new international energy trade contracts to export surplus electricity in the summer and import electricity in the winter.

7.6   CHECKS AND BALANCES

Before 2004, there were no checks and balances in the system at all, neither at a technical level nor at a financial level. No records were kept of the production or consumption of energy, neither by generation facilities nor by distribution companies. Special inter-agency teams were set up to check these figures, but most of the specialists were involved in the very bribery schemes they were tasked with detecting and eradicating. Private entities tried to maximize their profits at the expense of state-owned companies, while the managers of these companies were so poorly paid that they saw corrupt practices as the only way to make a decent living.

Making money on the side was generally not seen as criminal, or even immoral, but as inevitable. The system was so dysfunctional that there were many anecdotal cases when electricity generated by state-owned power plants was often credited to private power plants for some off-the-record cash reward to an official. The private power plant then proceeded to charge customers, most of which were also state-owned companies, for energy that had, in fact, been generated by the state in the first place. In other cases, officials credited private power plants with virtual energy generation that only served to create debts of a public company to the private entity. Parts of the proceeds were used to pay off the officials, while the rest went to private companies. The new government put an end to such schemes. Proper checks and balances, financial as well as technical, were introduced. Step by step, most of the sector was privatized, except for GSE and Enguri HPP. The remaining state-owned companies were put under new management, and the new managers were paid much higher salaries and bonuses to prevent corruption. Electronic meters with GSM systems were installed. These meters transmit readings to the central electronic hub every hour, a measure that makes it much easier to detect irregularities before they spin out of control. Black holes were closed, and clear rules were established. Unpaid bills, blackouts, capacity constraints, and debts to neighboring countries were a thing of the past.

7.7   Introduction of a Fact-Based Tariff System

During the very early stages of the reforms, tariffs covering the actual cost of production would have been counter-productive. While the collection rate was still low, law-abiding customers would have been unduly punished for their compliance. But once the collection rate hit 85 percent, the government sat down with GNERC, the independent regulator, to determine how distribution companies should set tariffs going forward. In 2005, the first tariff negotiations took place between privately held distribution companies and the Ministry of Energy. Many different aspects were taken into consideration: What were the technical needs of the grid itself, and what funds were needed for its full restoration? In what time frame? What was the policy of the ministry regarding the development of new generation facilities? Which parts of these facilities should be built by private distribution companies? What were the cash flow requirements? Once these questions were answered, a mutually acceptable tariff and a five-year investment program were agreed upon by the companies and the ministry. Thanks to these candid talks, relations between the government and the distributors reached a new, constructive level. The process and the mutual obligations it resulted in removed the uncertainty that previously hindered the development of the sector. I recommend conducting such tariff negotiations every five to seven years, starting two years before an existing five-year deal expires.

Subsequent to the negotiations, the parameters of the tariff scheme were submitted to GNERC, the regulator, for review and approval. While direct negotiations between the government and the distributor were important to clear away structural roadblocks, oversight by an independent body was no less important. Without an independent regulator, any government would be tempted to decrease tariffs before an election to win the favor of voters at the expense of the energy sector.

7.8   New Market Rules

The final stage of the reform of the energy sector in Georgia was launched in 2009, when the government introduced its new market rules. The objective of these rules was not to make a lot of changes that would only create uncertainty but to offer a long-term vision to all stakeholders, especially regarding the deregulation of the sector and the construction of new hydroelectric power plants. In 2009, only large customers, i.e., those who were connected to the high-voltage grid, were allowed to purchase electricity directly from generation companies. Everybody else had to buy their electricity from distribution companies. The government approved a 12-year plan, according to which the threshold for direct purchases would be decreased, step by step, to 1 kWh of consumption at the lowest voltage level by the year 2021. This gave distribution companies a more reliable planning perspective. It also increased the motivation for new private investors to build power plants. Additionally, small hydroelectric power plants (below a capacity of 13 MW) would not be regulated at all. They would be able to sell electricity at any price, while the prices were capped by the regulator for larger plants. The goal was to attract significant foreign direct investment to Georgia's energy sector.

Georgia has rivers with stable flows all year round, as well as sites fit for power generation near grid hubs and major roads. But because of past neglect, many of these sites remain undeveloped to this day. This is why constructing hydroelectric power plants in Georgia is only about half as costly as in other countries, where the best sites are already developed. What is more, the Georgian grid is well connected to its neighboring networks. As a result, there is high demand from international investors to build hydroelectric power plants in Georgia. The trouble was that, for a long time, the process of acquiring a license for construction was very complicated. It involved many government agencies, took a long time, and discouraged potential investors. You had to get approval for the site development from the Ministry of Energy and from the local authority for land acquisition or a land lease agreement. Additionally, you had to apply to the Ministry of the Environment for water usage rights and to the Ministry of Economy for construction. Connecting a new plant to the grid required approval by as many as three different agencies (GSE, PPA, and ESCO). The process was so complicated that nobody knew where even to start, or which paper they would have to get first. The new market rules radically simplified this process and put one entity – the Ministry of Energy – in charge of all government approval. In effect, power plant construction became almost a one-stop shopping affair for investors. All licenses and permits were coordinated by the Ministry of Energy on behalf of the investor. A memorandum of understanding obliged all government agencies to provide relevant documents to the investor through the Ministry of Energy. Today, the entire process takes a maximum of three months. In many other countries, that same process takes as long as two to three years. As a result, the Georgian energy sector has become one of the most attractive investment opportunities for private companies in the region, and it has already attracted billions of U.S. dollars in foreign direct investment to the country.

7.9   THE KAZBEGI CUCUMBER CASE

Fast-forward to the spring of 2016. We are in a meeting room at the Ministry of Energy in a Central Asian country. Participants include the minister and his deputy on one side of the table, representatives of the Asian Development Bank and me on the other side. The country is in a predicament closely resembling that in Georgia in the early 2000s. Their system has not been built to operate independently, but as a part of the bigger Soviet system. Most electricity generation is based on hydropower. Relations with the country's neighbors are difficult, causing problems with imports, high commercial losses, and accumulating debts. Our goal is to convince the minister that he is headed for a crash. We are certain that, without reform, the system will face serious difficulties within the next three to five years. Based on my experience, it is quite straightforward to calculate when the electricity system of any country will collapse. You don't even have to examine the technical conditions of the generation facilities and transmission assets in detail. All you have to do is look at the financials of the sector: Do the tariffs cover the actual cost of generation? If not, how big is the gap? What are the losses, commercial as well as technical? How fast is debt accumulating? Which other areas of the economy is the sector subsidizing with free or under-priced energy? How much funding does the government provide to the energy sector, if any?

If you study these figures for a period of five to seven years, you get a good understanding of where the sector is going and when it will grind to a halt. Georgia's energy sector was bankrupt in the late 1990s. It took another three to five years, until 2003, for it to collapse technically. While the situation in the country we were advising was not as bad as it had been in Georgia in the late 1990s, reforms were needed urgently, and I was specially brought in to share my experience in Georgia. Their biggest problem was cross-subsidization. The energy sector was subsidizing other parts of the economy, such as water utilities and agricultural entities. This is exactly what it had been like in Georgia when I took office there, and what it is still like today in many countries with electricity problems.

Here is how the conversation unfolded:

Minister: Even if we bring in management contractors from abroad, as you advise, we will have to keep using proceeds from the energy sector to subsidize water utilities and agriculture for political reasons.

Nika Gilauri: I fully understand. I was in the very same situation a few years ago. But the government is facing a simple choice: does it want to have electricity or not? If the government needs electricity, then the government has to pay for it. Even if the system has survived many years of underfinancing, it will not remain resilient forever. Also, I am guessing that some public customers are actually receiving more electricity than they really need. Believe me, I've seen it happen in my own country.

Minister: What is your suggestion?

Nika Gilauri: I am not saying that you should disconnect all the water utilities and all agricultural entities right away. First of all, let's calculate how much electricity they really need. Then let the government pay for this consumption. If they consume more, allow the electricity distribution company to disconnect the entity in question, or fire its manager. That can be the first step. But everybody has to understand that subsidizing the rest of the economy is not only your problem. It is a much bigger problem, and the government must deal with it.

The minister was not yet convinced. He liked the approach, but I felt a practical example was needed to show the real extent of the problem and illustrate how a small reform could turn out to make a big difference for his country. And that's when I remembered the cucumber story. It is a story set in our Kazbegi region, high in the Georgian mountains, at an altitude thousands of meters above sea level. As it happens, a high-pressure gas pipeline passes through the region. Sometime in the 1990s, the villagers had cut into the pipeline and started branching off gas. Initially, it was only a very small amount, and I believe it had even been approved by the government at the time. But year by year, the amount of gas diverted by these villages increased significantly. Of course, they were not paying for the gas. In the winter months, it is extremely difficult to get to the region, and collecting money in these remote villages was almost impossible. Eventually, special regulation was adopted, advocated by the member of parliament for that region. This regulation made it legal for the local population in high mountainous areas passed by high-pressure pipelines to divert gas – as if there were many such regions in Georgia, which is not the case. At some point in the 2000s, the amount of diverted gas had grown completely out of proportion with the number of households in the area. And still many people argued that a huge company like the GGTC (Georgina Gas Transportation Corporation) could afford to spare some gas for these villages. My argument at the time was very simple: if we want these villages to have gas for free, fine. But let's bring the deal out into the open, rather than have the energy sector bear the burden. Put a number on it, and let the government pay the GGTC for whatever energy these villages need.

When we investigated the root causes of the dramatic increase in consumption, it turned out that many Kazbegi locals had started to build greenhouses and cultivate cucumbers. By December 2004, every household in the region had at least one greenhouse and was using free gas to warm it up year-round, at an altitude of thousands of meters above sea level, where temperatures drop to –20 or even –30 degrees Celsius in the winter. Some households were said to run as many as half a dozen greenhouses. When a window of a greenhouse broke, they didn't bother fixing it. Rather, they simply increased the gas pressure. From their perspective, they were acting quite rationally. A new window would have cost them money, but gas was free. So my argument was to subsidize the gas, but openly and transparently: Let's calculate the value of the gas these villages really need, and let the Ministry of Finance pay the GGTC for it. When that decision was finally made after much debate, we sent a special team to the region to estimate how much gas was consumed by households for heating their homes and how much was consumed for commercial purposes. When we did the math, we found that the true cost of a single cultivated Kazbegi cucumber was more than GEL 20 (approximately USD 13). At the time, cucumbers were sold at GEL 2–3 per kilo. Our calculations showed that it would be cheaper to buy the greenhouses from the locals and have them dismantled, rather than keep on subsidizing the gas that was used to heat them. So that's what we did in 2005.

The cucumber story put a smile on the minister's face. He said that, in all probability, similar things were going on in his country. It remains to be seen what action he will take.

CHAPTER 8

Welfare – Focusing on the Neediest with a Simple Scoring Model

Abstract This chapter describes the introduction of a new welfare formula in Georgia that replaced a myriad of pre-existing social subsidies and tax breaks, many of which had been introduced to win the favor of voters prior to elections. These subsidies were flat and tied to all manner of products and services, from electricity to public transport, and they benefitted very different groups of people, from single mothers to war veterans. In a bold move, the new government froze most of these subsidies. To make sure that what little funds were available in the post-reform budget went to the neediest people, a scoring model for poverty based on property and living expenses was introduced. Based on this model the "[p]overty rates decreased from 21 percent in 2010 to less than 15 percent in 2012, and extreme poverty decreased from 7 percent in 2010 to 4 percent in 2012" (according to the Word Bank).

Keywords Poverty · Pension · Formula · Disproportionately · Benefits · Household

Corruption is already a thing of the past. The fiscal footprint of the state is cut down to size, providing stability and promoting long-term sustainability of the national economy. Taxes and customs are minimized, and the administration is streamlined to provide citizens and entrepreneurs with easy access to government agencies and institutions. Case closed? Not quite. One challenge remains: finding a way to ensure that government funds are used wisely to support the future growth and prosperity of the country, and the well-being of its citizens. It's not enough to take one smart decision, or ten, or a hundred. The real challenge is to embed sustainable financing of public services in public policy. In other words, the challenge is to trigger a virtuous cycle and build a legacy of smart spending.

8.1   WELFARE IN GEORGIA BEFORE 2004

At the turn of the millennium, Georgia was facing bankruptcy. This was largely due to the fact that a myriad of social subsidies and tax breaks had been introduced over time, usually to win the favor of voters prior to an election. These subsidies included all kinds of products and services, from gas and electricity to public transport and housing, and they were designed to benefit very different groups of people, from single mothers and large families to war veterans. In a bold move, the government transformed most of these flat subsidies into means-tested supports.[1] To make sure that what little funds were available in the post-reform budget went to the neediest people, a scoring model for poverty based on property and living expenses was introduced. In most cases, income was disregarded because it would have been too difficult to track, given that most low-paying jobs were part of the gray economy at the time. Based on this model, the new department of welfare singled out the 20 percent of the population that was most in need of assistance.

8.2   SOCIAL SUBSIDIES AS ELECTORAL BRIBES

Every country, be it developing or developed, piles up new types of welfare support with every election cycle. Before an election, every party comes up with new ideas for wealth redistribution to win the favor of the electorate. These ideas take different shapes (direct subsidies, tax credits, tax incentives), and they target different groups of voters, depending on whose votes are most contested in a given election. After the election, the winning party is under pressure to keep some, if not all, of its promises.

Fortunately, Otto von Bismarck was right when he said that "people never lie as much as after a hunt, during a war, and before an election."[2] If all pre-election promises to shower the electorate with wealth and favors were actually kept, many countries, if not the whole world, would long have gone bankrupt by now. Yet far too many welfare promises become a costly reality. Although such politically motivated subsidies are often a very inefficient means to fight poverty and promote prosperity, the next generation of politicians is usually hesitant to reduce or abolish any of them, lest they lose the favor of those who benefit from the subsidies. As a result, the subsidies remain in place until the next crisis. And it takes a really serious crisis to clean up the mess and put together a smart, efficient, well-balanced welfare system. And even if you get it done, chances are it won't last forever. With the next electoral cycle, the pile-up will start all over again. In this respect, a truly serious crisis is an opportunity. In the case of Georgia in the early 2000s, it was the imminent bankruptcy of the state that put the government in a position to start from scratch. Elsewhere, the opportunity might arise from a serious geopolitical challenge or a fundamental regime change, such as the introduction of a new form of government.

At the time, Georgia's welfare system consisted of dozens of different subsidies, tax breaks, and cash payouts to a wide and diverse range of beneficiaries. In fact, the Georgian welfare system was like a log of the country's history in many respects. It comprised cash support for veterans and family members of those who died in the Second World War, veterans and family members of those who died in the Soviet war in Afghanistan, veterans and family members of those who died in the war for the independence and sovereignty of Georgia (in the occupied territories of Abkhazia and the Tskhinvali region), for political victims of Soviet rule and members of their families, for people who suffered injuries at the hands of the Soviet army during the Tbilisi massacre in April 1989 and members of the families of those who died there, for those who went to Chernobyl after the nuclear reactor catastrophe, and displaced persons from Abkhazia or the Tskhinvali region. Additionally, there were social welfare benefits for various groups: single mothers, families with five or more children, people with physical disabilities (first, second, and third grade), and pensioners – men above the age of 65 and women above the age of 60. The full list was much longer, and there were additional healthcare subsidies for some of these groups.

8.3   Corruption and Inefficiency

On top of the cash payouts and healthcare subsidies, the Georgian welfare system comprised many non-cash subsidies for specific groups such as pensioners, students, and internally displaced persons. Examples include transport, electricity, gas, and schoolbooks. Finally, there were some tax and customs incentives. Cigarette imports, for instance, were exempt from customs payment for people with physical disabilities during a certain period. While the exemption may have been well intentioned at the time, it was quickly exploited by criminals. Suddenly, every importer was a disabled person. Of course, these individuals only acted as straw men for companies that did their business behind the scenes. Corruption was common in other areas as well. People bribed doctors to issue false disability certificates, or used the names of deceased family members to receive pensions, leading the authorities to believe that these pensioners were still alive. Others got even more creative and invented identities solely to swindle the government. Around 2007, the number of Second World War veterans started to increase, when it should, naturally have been decreasing as aging veterans passed away. Apparently, somebody had found "new" veterans who had eluded registration before. Of course, these claims turned out to be fraudulent.

The benefits often didn't reach those they were intended for, or at least not in full. And while the list of beneficiaries may sound plausible at first, the total number of those entitled to some sort of subsidy was so high that the amount received by a given family or individual was often shamefully small. For example, the average pension for the elderly only came to about USD 8–9 per month before 2004, and even that small sum was not paid by the government in full, or in time. Similarly, the monthly cash benefit for a disabled or internally displaced person was only USD 5–6, and that wasn't fully paid out either. On the flip side, some recipients didn't need the subsidies at all. For example, some displaced persons were wealthy individuals for whom the subsidies were a welcome but entirely unnecessary source of additional income.

In effect, the entire system was highly inefficient. It didn't reliably provide support to the neediest, and it awarded benefits to many people who didn't need them. The inadequacy of the system was apparent to all, but almost everybody had something to lose from fixing it, which is why Georgia had to get so close to bankruptcy for things to change.

8.4   INBUILT INERTIA

Even after the Rose Revolution, it was initially impossible to get rid of any subsidies, or even ward off the introduction of new benefits. How do you say no to single mothers and struggling families? Every time the new government went to parliament with a new budget, the opposition would argue that it's well and good to support families with more than five children, but why not support families with three or four children as well? Why not give more money to needy children directly? In the absence of a sound political culture – a big issue in many developing countries – the opposition does not have to come up with ways of financing such demands. Voters like what they hear, and it becomes even more difficult for any government to say no. In fact, this vicious cycle of demands and promises was one of the key drivers that brought Georgia to the brink of bankruptcy in early 2000's. This kind of vicious cycle is not at all uncommon. Similar systems are found in many other countries, developing as well as developed, and they are almost always plagued by corruption and inefficiency to some extent.

8.5   STARTING FROM SCRATCH WITH A SCORING MODEL

In Georgia, the financial situation got so serious that the government had no choice but to start from scratch and come up with an entirely new approach to social welfare. The only fair solution was, and still is, to identify the poorest segments of society and assist them, regardless of whether they are single mothers, families with five children, or displaced persons.

The governing idea was very simple. Georgia is not a rich country. It cannot afford to waste its resources on those who are relatively wealthy when many of the poor are going unassisted. Increasing taxes to finance social expenditure was out of the question because of the crisis the national economy was in. Any tax increase would have been disastrous for the newly developing private sector. The government had to minimize the inefficiencies and target the neediest with what little means it had. To this end, the government issued an announcement: "If you deem yourself poor, please register at the nearest government office to apply for assistance." Approximately 28 percent of all Georgians applied. Also, it quickly became obvious that some people had applied just to try their luck. For example, the list of applicants included some businessmen who were hoping for special tax breaks. A special department was created to develop a scoring model for all households.

It took a while to come up with a workable formula. The initial scoring model was mainly based on ownership, rather than income or expenses. This was because income was largely unregistered, especially for the poorest parts of society. Their income came from small-scale trade, from selling homegrown produce, or subsistence farming. The original list of line items that were incorporated into the formula included land, houses, apartments, and automobiles – all obviously relevant to determine, or at least approximate, someone's wealth from a property perspective. But the original list also included many other, less obvious items such as carpets, curtains, mobile phones, TV sets, and other electronic appliances. Many of these items were gifts from wealthier relatives, or had been left to families as part of an inheritance, which is why this approach caused significant frustration among the population. It took many iterations to develop a fairer formula. In the end, we settled on a formula essentially based on two pillars: proven property (land, house, apartment, and vehicle) and verifiable expenses (rent, mobile phone bill, electricity bill, and gas and water utility bill). Income is also part of the formula, but its weight is minimal as most of the prospective beneficiaries operated in the gray economy or had in-kind income, which made it impossible, or disproportionately difficult, to quantify their income in a reliable fashion.

The calculation of the welfare index for each applicant was based on the results of an interview conducted by a social worker, using a questionnaire that covered all the parameters used in the formula. The household welfare index was calculated according to the formula $I = C/N$, where C is a household consumption index and N is a household needs index. The lower the resulting welfare index, the lower the household welfare level. The household consumption index itself was calculated according to the following formula:

$$C = \exp\left(L_0 + \sum_{i=1}^{10} C_i \right)$$

In this formula, L_0 is a base coefficient. Summands C_1 through C_{10} are index values for parameters such as land use, livestock ownership, non-agricultural property, income, expenses, demography, education, skills, living conditions, and territory.[3]

A new department of welfare was created to implement the new formula. Many of its social workers were hired straight out of university. Every single application for social subsidies was checked, and often re-checked, to prevent any corrupt deals between government agents and applicants.

It turned out that approximately a quarter of the applicants did not meet the government's criteria for poverty, a wealth score below 120,000 points. While some entrepreneurs and owners of businesses had applied, hoping for special tax cuts or tax credits (as mentioned above) others were simply trying their luck. One family went so far as to take all furniture from one house to another. They submitted a forged rental agreement and showed the social worker around their empty house, claiming that they didn't own anything and didn't have any income. Ultimately, one-fifth of the population was identified as poor and, hence, entitled to some kind of financial assistance. Most of these households were already receiving some benefits from existing programs.

In the first year of the reform, it was decided that every household with a score below 57,000 would receive a cash benefit of approximately USD 20 per person per month. Why USD 20? Why every household with less than 57,000 points? Because this was exactly what was affordable within the limits of the budget at that time. All non-cash subsidies were abolished, and the funds that were freed up were used to finance the new, score-based cash program. The department of welfare gave money to the poorest and let them use it as they saw fit – on transportation, on utility payments, or on food, assuming that every individual is the best judge of what they need the most.

In the second phase, the same group of beneficiaries (members of households with a score below 57,000 points) received medical insurance vouchers on top of the cash assistance (see later in the text). In the third year, some 15 percent of households scoring between 57,000 and 70,000 points also received insurance vouchers. No cash benefits were awarded to this new group, as this would have exceeded the long-term financial means of the government. The ultimate test of any new measure was the long-term viability of the welfare system, irrespective of a given year's financial resources. The idea was, and still is, to verify the entitlement of beneficiaries on an annual basis by determining their scores, to give assistance only in cash, or in insurance vouchers, to the poorest as warranted by the long-term financial means of the government. Of course, it remains very difficult from a political perspective to remove any household from the list of beneficiaries, especially in an election year. This fact has weakened the reform, but the new system is still far superior to the preceding chaos. As a next step, the government may want to think about replacing the threshold-based approach with a sliding scale allocation of assistance (i.e., cash paid out in direct proportion to a household's score). This will put an end to relative injustices, such as a household with the score of 56,999 receiving the full assistance and another one, with a score of 57,001, not receiving anything.

The new formula was first introduced in Georgia in 2006. It had many flaws, and many mistakes were made; but as a result of continuous improvements to the formula and to its administration, the results were outstanding. Of course, Georgia's overall economic growth also helped. According to the World Bank, the Georgian welfare program was one of the most successful in the world in terms of targeting the neediest: "Poverty rates decreased from 21 percent in 2010 to less than 15 percent in 2012, and extreme poverty decreased from 7 percent in 2010 to 4 percent in 2012."[4]

Despite the very successful reform, some subsidies survived. The plan was to phase them out over time. However, during the next political cycle, some former subsidies were resurrected, e.g., the subsidy of public transport for pensioners. I still believe that the welfare reform conducted in Georgia between 2006 and 2010 was very successful, and that many countries would benefit from introducing similar systems. The central idea is as simple as it is powerful: put an end to a myriad of subsidies and non-cash flat benefits to different, partly random groups of beneficiaries. Instead, identify the neediest, categorize them based on their financial means, and provide them with cash assistance to the extent that the government can afford. Let the neediest decide how to spend these funds. Stay away from non-cash flat subsidies or tax breaks that will often make the rich richer, rather than help the poor. For example, if the government subsidizes gas (petrol), those who consume the most – drivers of sports cars, or owners of a fleet of trucks – will benefit the most.

When the government of Georgia went to parliament with the new system, it was easy to counter the opposition's questions and demands with fact-based replies: "Yes, we provide welfare assistance to single mothers, as well as to families with five or more children. In fact, we even help families with two or three children. We give assistance to people with disabilities, and they get more than they did in the past. But we give money only to those families who need the assistance the most. Georgia cannot afford to give money to rich people with disabilities, or to rich families with seven children." Politically, getting parliamentary approval for a new budget, or any type of reform, had never been easier.

Notes

1. No new beneficiaries were accepted into these programs. Existing beneficiaries were given a choice to keep receiving the old subsidies or to upgrade to the new formula, which resulted in higher total payments. Of course, everybody chose the new welfare program. Effectively, most of the old subsidies seized to exist.
2. Im neuen Reich: Wochenschrift für das Leben des deutschen Volkes in Staat, Wissenschaft und Kunst, Band 1; Band 9; Verlag von S. Hirzel, 1879, p. 199.
3. *Household welfare level evaluation methodology*, internal document available through the author.
4. http://www.worldbank.org/en/results/2014/04/15/supporting-inclusive-growth-and-development-in-georgia (retrieved in April 2014).

CHAPTER 9

Healthcare – Unleashing the Power of Public-Private Partnership

Abstract This chapter describes how the government partnered with private enterprises to renew the country's healthcare system. Before the reforms, health insurance was a foreign concept for the vast majority of Georgians. In 2006, less than 1 percent of the population was insured. At the same time, most healthcare facilities were in a state of ill repair, and the medical staff was insufficiently trained. In response, the government divided the country into healthcare clusters and requested bids from insurance companies to provide basic coverage for the neediest in a given cluster. The winning bidder was obligated to renovate or rebuild and operate the hospitals in that area. By 2012, more than half the population was insured and more than 150 new or renovated hospitals were opened. What is more, competition between providers also resulted in higher incentives for medical personnel to perform well and grow professionally.

Keywords Insurance · Healthcare · Public-private partnerships · Obamacare · Special insurance program (SIP)

Until recently, health insurance was an unfamiliar concept for the vast majority of Georgians. In 2006, less than 1 percent of the population was insured. Most healthcare facilities were in a state of ill repair, and the medical staff was insufficiently trained. In response, the government

© The Author(s) 2017
N. Gilauri, *Practical Economics*,
DOI 10.1007/978-3-319-45769-7_9

divided the country into healthcare clusters and invited bids from insurance companies to provide basic coverage for the neediest in a given cluster. The winning bidder was mandated to renovate or rebuild and operate the hospitals in that area. The scheme, set up as one of Georgia's biggest public-private partnerships to date, was a big success. By 2012, more than half of the population was insured. What is more, competition between providers also resulted in better service for patients and in higher incentives for medical personnel to perform well and grow professionally.

9.1   THE SOLIDARITY CHALLENGE

Worldwide, governments have come up with various approaches to tackle healthcare. Even developed countries are struggling to find the right setup. The latest, and perhaps most prominent, experiment to bring affordable healthcare to the masses is "Obamacare" in the United States. It is widely criticized, and the jury is still out on its long-term impact. The underlying challenge is one of solidarity. The young and healthy are reluctant to spend much on insurance; they regard it as a waste of money. But any insurance system solely dependent on contributions from the elderly and infirm alone will have a funding problem. And few governments, except perhaps for those in countries with valuable natural resources, can afford to finance healthcare without some form of continuous contribution from the population. What is more, completely free healthcare is an incentive for patients to collude with providers and request treatment beyond what is necessary. If healthcare is fully paid for, corrupt individuals will always find a way to take advantage of the system by charging the government extra costs. When they are confronted, they will manipulate public opinion by saying that the government is cutting corners at the expense of the well-being of the population.

In Georgia, the problems in 2009 went beyond this fundamental financing challenge. Most healthcare facilities had been built in the 1960s and 1970s and were not properly maintained because of insufficient funds. Much medical equipment was outdated, hospitals were overstaffed, but most medical personnel were not sufficiently trained. While the approach the government came up with may not have solved all of these structural problems at once, it was still a big step in the right direction for the healthcare system in Georgia.

9.2   THE SPECIAL INSURANCE PROGRAM

In 2010, the Georgian government started its "special insurance program" (SIP). In parallel, state-owned healthcare facilities were privatized. All facilities were categorized based on a single question: were they commercially viable? If they were, they were to be privatized right away. If they weren't, they were either kept under state ownership (e.g., essential clinics to treat infective diseases) or made part of the second stage of the SIP, although that second stage was never fully implemented.

The SIP was a joint effort by the state and all private insurance companies; Georgia did not have any public or state-owned insurance companies. Its primary target group was that part of the population that had been identified by the welfare program as most in need (see previous chapter). At the first stage of the SIP, the government defined the minimum insurance package and gave insurance vouchers covering that minimum package to the neediest families. Families were free to redeem their voucher for minimum coverage with any of the private insurance companies. All monthly payments were picked up by the government. The fact that the group of those insured under this scheme did not only include the elderly or the sick but everyone in the lowest wealth bracket made the voucher relatively cheap; initial calculations regarding the package and the price of the voucher were carried out by the Ministry of Healthcare in consultations with actuaries and private insurance companies.

9.3   INITIAL SETBACKS

Unfortunately, the government's expectation that the scheme would create competition among insurance companies and increase the quality of service, or encourage companies to offer additional services beyond the minimum package, did not come true. The miscalculation the government made was to assume that the poorest had sufficient knowledge of what insurance was and that they would not trade the voucher for cash. While vouchers were numbered and named to prevent beneficiaries from selling their vouchers to others, there was no mechanism in place to stop insurance companies from offering cash instead of better service in exchange for the vouchers. As a result, many of the neediest effectively sold their vouchers to insurance companies rather than redeem them for improved service or extended coverage. Companies even employed so-called "marketing" agents that would go door to door and offer cash in exchange for the voucher.

Competing companies adopted different "marketing" approaches. Some of them hired local doctors as their representatives, while others hired school-teachers, who were opinion leaders in many rural areas at the time. Some even went as far as enlisting the services of representatives of local governments to attract as many voucher holders as possible. For an insurance company, the voucher was a guarantee of steady income from the government. This made it well worth the comparatively small expense of a cashback to voucher holders, most of whom had no idea how the system worked.

At the time, the whole concept of insurance was completely new for Georgia. Most Georgians only had a vague idea how they would benefit from being insured. The government ran an extensive communications campaign to educate the population about these benefits, but the campaign failed to reach most of its target audience. The insurance companies took advantage of the ignorance of many voucher holders and made the cash kickback the norm. The poor preferred to give their vouchers to those companies that offered cash in exchange, rather than to those who offered better service or coverage. The government's plan to define the basic insurance package and then have private insurance companies compete with each other by offering additional services to voucher holders failed.

9.4   HEALTHCARE CLUSTERS

To put an end to the semi-corrupt practices, the government devised a large-scale public-private partnership program, pursuing a dual objective: provide healthcare services to the poor and build new, state-of-the-art healthcare facilities, or upgrade existing facilities. As a first step, the whole country was divided into relatively small healthcare clusters. For each cluster, the government determined the number of necessary hospital beds as well as the number of voucher recipients. As a next step, the government announced a tender among private insurance companies for every cluster to insure all voucher holders in that cluster. The winning company would be required to build new hospitals (or renovate existing hospitals which were transfered from state to the insurance company for free) as deemed necessary for that cluster within 18–24 months, equipped with state-of-the-art technology as specified by the Ministry of Healthcare, and adjust the number and qualification of medical employees.

An auction was held in each cluster, and the contract went to the company that offered the lowest cost per insured person. In most clusters, the government signed over the existing hospital to the winning company – complete with land, buildings, equipment, and staff – for free. The company would then have to refurbish or re-build, re-equip, and re-staff the hospital. In the vast majority of cases, the existing infrastructure was in such a poor repair that only the land could be used.

Except for insufficiently qualified employees who lost their jobs, everybody won:

- *The state.* The government successfully privatized healthcare facilities that had been mismanaged before: hospitals that were overstaffed, did not provide adequate service, yet kept asking for additional funds from the government. The most difficult decision – to reduce inefficiency and let go part of the medical personnel – was shifted to private sector players, who took care of it efficiently and effectively.
- *Private insurance companies.* Insurers received additional funds for the insured and were given an opportunity to enter a new market, effectively becoming healthcare providers. The transformation was co-financed through the PPP program. All the insurance companies had to do was to calculate the costs of the facilities they would be required to build, add these costs to the cost of providing insurance services to the insured in the specific cluster, and come up with the price per insured individual.[1]
- *Medical staff.* While the total number of hospital employees shrunk, those who stayed were given higher salaries (based on their performance), a better work environment, better training, and better equipment to work with.
- *Patients.* The population was given much better service in newly built or fully refurbished hospitals. One hundred fifty new hospitals were put into operation over the course of 18 months, some of them newly built, others newly renovated.

As a whole, the resulting contracts constituted one of the biggest public-private partnerships between the government and private sector in Georgia.

In Tbilisi, the capital, the situation was slightly different. The privatization tender was held among insurance companies only to insure the poor, not to build any new hospitals, as a different hospital development plan was put together for the capital city. Tbilisi itself was also broken down into clusters, and every hospital was privatized based on open tenders or bought out by the existing staff. Where there was a lack of interest from the private sector, the government adopted a different approach. The Ministry of Healthcare itself refurbished some buildings and gave them to state-owned hospitals under the condition that the staff would buy out these hospitals at a minimum price per square meter, payable in installments, and bring in new equipment. Despite initial disputes, a few dozen hospitals were privatized in this fashion and moved to newly renovated buildings.

9.5   HUMAN RESOURCE DEVELOPMENT

Of course, the cluster-based partnership with private companies did not solve every problem overnight. Training was the biggest challenge. The level of training medical personnel had previously received was very low. The new setup provided a better environment for them to grow professionally. In the past, most of the hospitals had been owned by the state. There was no competition among the hospitals and, hence, no need to attract and develop the best doctors. The privatization of most of the hospitals brought competition for patients, and this triggered a war for talent too. Hospitals made investments to attract the best doctors and to improve the qualification of their medical personnel.

Many healthcare experts believe in the magic of regulation and pre-reform Georgia was no exception. Regulation and licensing was widely regarded as the key to highly qualified staff. While this might work in some countries, it didn't work in Georgia. Because of corrupt practices and government inefficiencies, the regulatory approach was not effective. Only the introduction of competition among different healthcare providers brought a significant improvement. When the state is the only (or main) provider of healthcare and salaries of doctors are regulated, doctors have no incentive to invest in their professional development. The income gap between the best doctor and the worst one usually does not reflect the relative levels of their qualification and performance. Often, regulated salaries are tied to tenure rather than performance. Good doctors are irked by this injustice and often develop their own private practice, partly illegally, alongside their duties as state employees in public hospitals. Less ambitious doctors simply stop making an effort to grow professionally or provide superior service to patients. This effect can, to some extent, be compensated for with performance-based bonuses, but many countries have not introduced such schemes to the healthcare sector. But if the healthcare sector is privatized and companies are under pressure to attract the best personnel, doctors have an incentive to perform well, to grow professionally, and to make names for themselves in their respective areas of specialization. This is exactly what happened in Georgia since the reforms outline previously.

Privatization also helped to take care of a problem that was quite specific to Georgia. Georgians are naturally proud. Everybody wants to be a doctor, and nobody wants to be a nurse. And as the healthcare sector was just as corrupt as any other sector in pre-reform Georgia, most of the medical staff could simply buy a doctor's license. As a result, Georgia had more doctors than nurses before the privatization of the healthcare sector. But the managers of the private companies that participated in the cluster-based auctions knew very well that they would have no use for vast numbers of insufficiently trained, questionably licensed doctors. Some of them were let go, and some of them volunteered to retrain with special programs.

9.6   RESOLVING CONFLICTS OF INTEREST

Eventually, a new problem arose from a structural conflict of interest. In most clusters, hospital operations and insurance were in the hands of the same company. Without proper precautions, this could easily have resulted in poor service. Especially in rural areas, insurance companies were tempted to cash in on their privilege as the only provider of healthcare services and maximize profits by providing inadequate service. The government used a combination of three measures to prevent this from happening:

- *Granularity.* The clusters were defined in a way that made it easy for private patients to go to a competitor's hospital in the neighboring cluster. Since most companies were trying to serve not only state-insured patients but private patients as well, this acted as a powerful incentive to provide good service.
- *Protocols.* Additionally, the government put in place protocols that specify the minimum service level and a price for that level of service. These protocols were based on international best practices and local price levels. Beneficiaries who choose to obtain medical services from a private provider pay the difference between the price specified by the protocol and the private bill.
- *Supervision.* Finally, the medical regulator was strengthened to help resolve three types of potential conflict: customers dealing with insurance companies, hospitals dealing with insurance companies, and hospitals dealing with customers.

Specifically, the regulator protects beneficiaries from local monopolies, i.e., areas in which the hospital owned by the insurance company is the only medical facility. If there are numerous complaints from beneficiaries in a given cluster, the regulator will conduct an investigation and, if need be, annul the license of any hospital or any doctor. The regulator also has the authority to force an insurance company to allow beneficiaries to go to another hospital if they are willing to pay the difference between the protocol price and the price asked by the competing hospital. And the regulator has a right to resolve disputes between an insurance company and a hospital, typically regarding delayed payments from insurance companies to hospitals.

Protocols and regulatory oversight also partially helped to take care of one of the last remaining issues in Georgia's healthcare sector at the time: the cost of emergency surgery. Under the new scheme, emergency surgery carries a higher price tag than planned procedures. When this regulation took effect, the number of emergency heart operations increased threefold, while the number of planned heart operations decreased accordingly. Doctors were simply filling out the forms in a way that would maximize their profits. Protocols and strict regulatory oversight was an attempt to prevent these practices. However, practice showed that the only way for minimizing the abuse of state financing in the healthcare is 80/20 co-financing structure of the insurance scheme. The co-financing must be done at the moment of receiving healthcare services, not necessarily during obtaining insurance packages. For the poorest, additional financing scheme must be put in place that subsidizes most of the 20 percent co-financing obligation. Only with co-financing scheme the patient has all the right incentives not to follow proposed schemes of the hospitals and carefully study the costs rather than feel free to let the doctors work their documents to earn more money on the back of state finances.

9.7   THE END STATE

In 2012, the status of the Georgian healthcare system was as follows. With the exception of the capital, the vast majority of hospitals was privatized and managed by one of the five major insurance companies that had participated in the cluster-based auctions. A handful of healthcare facilities had been singled out as not commercially viable but medically indispensable. Examples include an HIV clinic, a treatment center for infective diseases, and a tuberculosis clinic. The government decided to keep these facilities under state ownership and provide them with additional funds to update their infrastructure and improve the service.

By 2012, the five insurance companies had already built or fully renovated more than 100 hospitals. The size of these hospitals varied, depending on the healthcare requirements in a given cluster. Most hospitals were small (10–25 beds), but there were also a few larger ones with more than 50 beds. In some regions, other private providers emerged and started competing with the hospitals operated by the five insurance companies. In some cases, these new competitors were the successors of decommissioned former state-owned hospitals that had been bought out by their staff, an approach similar to the process that had been adopted in Tbilisi. By the end of 2012, there were more than 20 companies that owned hospitals across Georgia. Some of them big, some of them small, some of them offering universal healthcare, others specialized in one way or another. By 2012, most of the unnecessary staff in the healthcare sector had already been laid off. Competition among hospitals for the best doctors was fierce, and doctors were highly motivated to grow professionally. Many of them participated in specially devised training programs.

In 2006, less than 1 percent of Georgian population had health insurance. By the end of 2012, more than half of the population was insured. About 25 percent of the insured were privately participating in the SIP, while the rest was covered by the government's basic insurance policy. The insurance policy covered all medical expenses for the poor, 80 percent of the cost of medical treatment for everybody else and 50 percent of the cost of drugs (up to USD 100 USD per year). The 80-percent coverage turned out to yield the best tradeoff between service quality and efficiency. It discourages beneficiaries from receiving unnecessary services and helps minimize collusion between doctors and patients to cheat the insurer.

Most recently, the Georgia Healthcare Group (GHG) went public on the London Stock Exchange. At the time of the IPO in November 2015, the company had been in the healthcare business for less than a decade. But thanks to good management and favorable conditions in Georgia's healthcare market, the IPO was a big success.

9.8   LATER DEVELOPMENTS

The original plan was to liberalize the healthcare sector completely at the next stage. Once insurance companies had recovered their investments in newly built hospitals, the cluster system should have been dismantled, allowing all voucher holders to choose any insurance company, depending on who offers the best service. Thanks to a much more knowledgeable population, it might have worked the second time round. The government elected in 2012, however, chose a different path and decided to insure every citizen of Georgia, regardless of wealth and age – a bold and a popular move, but it remains to be seen whether the effects of this move will financially sustainable in a long term.[2]

In any case, the reforms undertaken between 2010 and 2012 are widely recognized as a major breakthrough moment for the Georgian healthcare sector, especially for the population, who now receives better and more reliable treatment than ever before in the country's history.

NOTES

1. Actually, due to their lack of experience, some of the private companies miscalculated the revenue streams and had to be merged with others to absorb the impact. Some even went bankrupt.
2. http://www.georgiapolicy.org/2016/03/georgia-is-moving-forward-on-welfare-reform/ (retrieved in May 2016).

CHAPTER 10

Education – School Financing and University Reform

Abstract This chapter tells the story of how Georgia's government reformed higher education in Georgia by diverting the flow of financing from institutions, such as schools and universities, to customers, i.e., students and their parents. Prior to the reform, many institutions were underfunded, and almost all teachers were underpaid. Under the new scheme, students were given vouchers that could be redeemed at any school. This created healthy competition among providers, and it improved the quality of education dramatically. Additionally, a system was put in place under which government bonuses were awarded for performance, as measured by student achievements in university entrance exams and school final exams, as well as for teacher proficiency and certification. The chapter concludes with a discussion of the plan to establish an American University in Georgia.

Keywords Education · School system · Exams · Computer-aided tests (CAT) · Voucher-based

10.1   School Reform – Diverting the Flow of Financing from Schools to Students

Education reform is frequently neglected by politicians, simply because any given cohort of students will see several election cycles before they leave the system. In Georgia, many schools were underfunded, and almost all teachers were underpaid in the early 2000s. As a result, degrees

© The Author(s) 2017
N. Gilauri, *Practical Economics*,
DOI 10.1007/978-3-319-45769-7_10

and diplomas were for sale to the highest bidder. In response, the new government diverted the flow of financing: from schools to students and their parents. Students were given vouchers that could be redeemed at any school. This created healthy competition among providers, and it improved the quality of schooling dramatically. Additionally, a bonus system was put in place to reward schools for good performance.

10.1.1   The Long Haul

No country can prosper for any length of time without making continuous improvements and upgrades to its education system. Teachers are, perhaps, the most important enablers of a better future in any country. They are also opinion leaders in almost all developing countries, on par with medical doctors. For a lot of people, especially in rural areas, teachers are the incarnation of authority. Says J.D. Salinger: "You can't stop a teacher when they want to do something. They just do it."[1] At the same time, many teachers are politically very active. This means that any reform of the education system in a developing country almost automatically leads to political turmoil.

To make things even more difficult, it takes a long time until education reform yields visible effects. Reforms in most other areas have a much shorter lead time, a clear political advantage. Typically, almost any reform initially faces more opposition than support. Most people get attached to the status quo, be it good or bad. To win the favor of these people, reformers need to produce positive results quickly, ideally within a year or two. But it takes a decade for education reform to deliver real, initial results. This timeframe exceeds the average political cycle by a factor of two. As a result, politicians are reluctant to tackle education reform: most teachers won't like the changes, whatever they may be, and those who benefit won't feel the advantages the reform brings until it's too late for those who introduce the changes to bring in the harvest. As a result, transforming the education system is arguably one of the biggest political challenges of all, in developing as well as developed countries.

10.1.2   Bribes over Brains

To graduate from school with good grades and be accepted by a university in pre-reform Georgia, students needed money and connections, rather than brains or hard work. This was due to two fundamental flaws in Georgia's school system in the early 2000s: teachers were generally underpaid, and schools were generally overstaffed.

- *Salaries for teachers were very low.* As in many other areas of public service, this gave rise to widespread corruption. Teachers had no choice but to make money on the side to provide for themselves and their families.
- *The number of teachers was too high.* There simply were not enough other jobs, and being a teacher was better than being unemployed. Teaching may not have been well paid, but at least it came with a certain social status.

There were three types of teachers: good, bad, and independent. The good ones made additional income by giving private lessons after school and helping students prepare for exams. The bad ones made additional income by accepting bribes or gifts from parents in exchange for good grades. The independent ones, a very rare type, were those whose families were wealthy enough to let them pursue teaching as a calling. But generally, the pay was so low that most teachers were involved in some sort of illegal activity to make money on the side. As a result, it was virtually impossible even for a gifted, hard-working student to pass a university entrance exam without paying a bribe or taking advantage of personal connections, while underachievers from well-connected, wealthy families had no trouble getting accepted. The effect on the morale and motivation of a whole generation of young people was disastrous. Their dreams of a better future for themselves and for their country were crushed by corruption.

10.1.3   Getting Started

The Georgian government had to choose where to start the education reform process: At the primary level? In the secondary school system? At universities? In teachers' preparation courses? We started somewhere else – with university entrance exams, the nexus of secondary schools and universities. It quickly became clear that it was the right choice. The reform produced fast results and gave the government political credit for further reforms. Most importantly, it got students to believe that they have a future, and that it pays to study and work hard, even if you don't have connections. Initially, however, the reform faced fierce opposition because the corrupt practices had provided many employees in the education system with illegal income for so many years. But since the victims of these practices were even more numerous than the beneficiaries, there was immediate and overwhelming support for this reform in the population. The government relieved universities of their right to hold entrance exams. To ensure that universities could not jeopardize the reform, no leakage of any information was to be tolerated. It worked. In line with international best practice, the government created an independent, central examinations center. All over the country, applicants took the same exams simultaneously. The year 2005 was the first year in which all students got into tertiary education institutions without paying bribes for better grades and having patrons in high positions make phone calls to admission officers. In the first year, almost nobody believed that it was actually a free and fair process. Because of the many years of bad experience, everybody suspected that everybody else got better grades than they deserved. But after the second year, the centralization of entrance exams was already one of the top-rated reforms. Students started to study at schools to prepare themselves for the exams and for a better future. Studies show that students from poor regions were the biggest winners of the reform. Later on, computer-aided tests (CAT) were introduced to make the process easier to administer, protect the results from manual interference, and gain even more trust.

10.1.4   School Financing: Money Follows Students

As a next step, the government tackled school financing. Before the reform, funding received by schools very much depedned on personal relations between school principles and Ministry of Education. Almost all parameters, even the number of teachers assigned to a given school, were pre-approved by the ministry. This system led to a vicious cycle of corruption. School directors shared their funds with the very government officials who green-lighted their budgets, a system that is still common today in many developing countries.

The reform was simple in essence. In the past, money had gone to the schools. In the future, money would go to students. Students and their parents were given total freedom to choose a school, be it public or private, anywhere in the country, regardless of the school district in which they lived. No regional assignments or privileges were given to any school. Every student received a voucher from the government, and the school chosen by the student would receive the cash value of the voucher from the state's education budget. Most students chose a school nearby, which is why most of the ensuing competition was regional. But in some cases, especially in cities, students flocked to a few reputable schools. To avoid overcrowding, the number of students that each school could accept was limited. This cap was based on the space the school had. First-year students were selected on a "first come, first served" basis. Electronic applications helped avoid corrupt deals. This reform created healthy competition among schools. Many schools hired better teachers because they realized that students and their parents followed the best teachers, and that funds would follow the students.

The most important feature of this reform was that students were allowed to take their vouchers not only to public schools but to private schools as well, and that budgetary funds were subsequently transferred to these private schools. Although the value of the voucher was too low to pay for an education at most private schools in full and needed to be topped up by students' parents, the overall effect was one of healthy competition. It gave rise to many high-caliber new schools. Over the course of less than three years, the share of private schools as a percentage of the total number of schools jumped from 1.5 percent to 14 percent.

To determine the value of a voucher for a given student, the Ministry of Education developed a special formula. Initially, there were three basic variations of the formula, depending on where the student lived: in an urban area, in a rural area, or in a mountainous area. This was to account for the fact that the cost of running a school is typically higher in rural and mountainous areas because of smaller average class sizes. Additionally, schools in the mountains have to deal with higher expenses for heating because of the cold winters. Had the value of the voucher been the same for everyone, schools outside urban areas would have been underfunded.

10.1.5   *The Black Hole*

Having the money follow customers, i.e., students and their parents, rather than institutions, was a key catalyst to reduce inefficiencies and drive improvements. Yet the new system faced three challenges, all of them related to the fact that the demand side of the school system was liberalized, but the supply side was not. While students were free to choose any school they wanted, schools were not able to adjust their offering to the shifting needs of students.

- *Overstaffing*. School directors quickly realized that they could not afford to keep on teachers who were not productive. But at the time, it was difficult for schools to let anyone go. Most schools were still state-owned institutions, and school directors wanted the government to take responsibility for any lay-offs. A handful of schools, however, managed to adjust their staff numbers without external intervention. As a result, they were able to increase the salaries of high-performing teachers.
- *Oversupply*. In some urban areas, there were far too many schools relative to the number of students. Partly, this was due to demographic changes. But since some of these schools had been established for political reasons in the first place, or as part of corrupt deals sealed in the past, it was difficult to close them down. This part of the school reform was very unpopular, but it was indispensable to implement the reform without breaking the budget.
- *Underfunding*. Although the value of the voucher reflected different levels of operating cost, some schools were not sustainable based on voucher funding alone. This mostly affected schools in remote areas that were the only provider of higher education for miles around and could, hence, not be closed down, even if the number of students was very low. Such schools were designated as "deficit schools" and received additional financing from the Ministry of Education.

This last challenge increased over time. In the first year of the reform, only 20 percent of all schools were designated as so-called deficit schools. But two years later, more than 50 percent had been designated deficit schools. As soon as school directors realized that the "deficit school" designation gave them access to additional financing, they got creative and found ways to meet the criteria. For example, some directors simply hired new teachers, often their relatives and friends. Others launched costly renovation programs. And all of them came to the Ministry of Education in the middle of winter to request heating subsidies. How do you say no to children who are without heating in the middle of winter? The government had no choice but to provide additional direct funding from the budget. Unfortunately, these exceptions had a snowball effect. The more schools were awarded additional financing, the more came up with new emergencies in an illicit competition for funds on top of the value of the vouchers. A black hole had formed in the education budget, and it was growing.

10.1.6   Reforming the Reform

After a little over two years, it became apparent that the reform was failing. It's not unusual. One-off reforms rarely work. The hallmark of successful transformations is continuous improvement. So the government devised further changes, effectively reforming the reform. As a first step, the formula used to calculate the voucher value was refined. The new formula recognizes a wide range of factors that influence the cost of schooling in a given student's area of residence, such as the size of the nearest school, its offering beyond the standard curriculum, and its location:

$$V = b + \sum_{i=1}^{7} vi$$

V is the total cash value of the voucher. While b is the base value (GEL 300 per student per year), summands v_1 through v_7 cover surcharges for operating cost, the number of students, curriculum development, inclusion education, school maintenance, remote locations, and teachers' bonuses.

Additional funds were set aside for voucher funding so that voucher-based payments would cover the cost of running any school. As a result, the special status of a "deficit school" was eliminated. From then on, no school director could go to the Ministry of Education for additional non-voucher funding.

As a second step, the government decided to help school directors reduce the number of teachers. There had been far too many teachers, even before the initial reform. But because of the unhealthy competition among schools for additional funding from the "black hole," the number of teachers had ballooned to a ludicrous level. In 2010, the ratio of teachers to students in Georgia was one of the highest in the world. According to data gathered by the World Bank, there was one teacher for every nine students in Georgia in 2010. The global average that year was 25. Only four countries had even fewer students per teacher than Georgia: Bermuda, Kuwait, Liechtenstein, and San Marino.[2] The extra teachers cost Georgia a fortune, caused systemic inefficiency, and had a negative impact on the motivation of good teachers. They had to go – a suicide mission for any government. And in fact, the first attempt to lay them off backfired.

The government had decreed that every teacher needed to be certified by 2014. In order to be certified, every teacher would have to pass an exam. To motivate teachers to take the exam sooner rather than later, teachers were awarded special bonuses for passing the exam and additional bonuses for proven computer literacy and certified English language skills.

Why should a Georgian teacher of, say, biology have English language skills? The idea was simple. If you speak English, you can use international sources to keep abreast of developments in your discipline and help prepare students from a small country to make their way in the world. Ultimately, it's about widening one's horizon. Georgia had been occupied by Russia for many years. At the time, almost everybody over the age of 30 spoke Russian. In a situation like that, having a teacher who (also) speaks English is an important stepping-stone for students to develop an open-minded worldview.

Despite its inherent logic, the decision to build English language skills into the certification and bonus scheme for teachers, as well as the very idea of certification itself, caused major political turmoil. The problem was not so much the carrot. The problem was the stick. Initially, teachers were allowed to take the certification exam only once, and if they failed, they were let go. Teachers took to the streets in protest, saying that they had worked as teachers for decades, helped raise generations of children, and should not lose their livelihood based on the result of a single exam. And they were right. The government reacted quickly and introduced a less restrictive certification scheme. Teachers now had the right to take the certification exam three times over the course of a two-year period. Additionally, every teacher was entitled to one free preparation course. Only teachers who failed the exam all three times were let go. Within two years of the introduction of this new regulation, the number of teachers went down by 25 percent, and no more complaints were heard. In fact, teachers who failed three times were so ashamed that they often chose to leave schools on personal grounds rather than waiting for their contracts to be annulled because of their lack of certification. This particular element of Georgia's school reform is a fine example of how a failing reform can be turned into a success story by swift and decisive adjustments to the initial plan.

In a third step, the government created a new motivational system for school directors. Every school was ranked according to the average achievements of its students in the new, centralized university entrance exams, or in final school exams – this later reform could only be implemented once centralized, computer-aided exams had been introduced throughout the country. Having schools administer exams locally would only have caused additional corruption. Using these existing indicators was not only easier, and more transparent, than introducing an additional assessment, it also reflected the number one pursuit of students and their parents: better performance in final school exams or university entrance exams. At the time, the ranking was already being published, and parents used this as a guide when picking schools for their children. As a result, high-performing schools attracted more students and received more voucher-based financing than their low-performing peers. To increase this effect, the government rewarded the directors of the top 10 percent schools with substantial bonuses, while the directors of the bottom 10 percent schools were laid off and replaced. As a next step, directors should have received additional funds to reward high-performing teachers, but this stage of the reform was not implemented.

Georgia's experience with a school's average performance in university entrance exams as the reference metric for performance-based funding was overwhelmingly positive. But not all countries have comparable entrance exams. Alternative indicators that can be used to assess a school's performance and provide corresponding rewards include schools' final exams, students' achievements in science olympics, essay-writing contests, or other competitive events overseen by independent institutions. Using such objective criteria will encourage school directors to invest as much of their funds as possible in the *de facto* quality of the education they provide, rather than in marketing or other non-core activities. This is relevant even in developed countries, where schools have a tendency to spend more money on advertising at the expense of teachers' salaries and school infrastructure.

10.1.7 Results

After many years of reforms, some mistakes, and a fair number of innovations, Georgia now has a highly efficient, results-oriented system of school financing:

- *Funds follow students, not schools.* This creates competition among schools to attract more students by providing a better education – better teachers, better facilities, and better materials.
- *Students are free to choose any school.* The fact that vouchers can be redeemed at any school, disregarding school districts, including private schools, fosters the improvement of individual schools and creates even more competition. Teachers are motivated to grow

professionally to qualify for employment at private schools that typically pay higher salaries than public schools.

- *Schools receive bonuses for performance.* Schools are assessed based on the performance of their students in university entrance exams. Directors of top-performing schools are given additional funds, while directors of low-performing schools are counselled to leave.

10.1.8   Broken English

Around the same time, the Ministry of Education also launched its campaign to increase the number of native speakers teaching English in Georgian schools. There were very few English teachers in Georgia to begin with, and their knowledge was theoretical, based on Russian textbooks, rather than practical experience. For a long time, Russian had been the only foreign language taught in Georgian schools. It was clear that Georgia needed a step change in this area to prepare its students for life in a globalized world with English as its *de facto lingua franca.*

The Ministry of Education ran a communication campaign to explain why learning English mattered, emphasizing that only students who speak English would eventually be able to compete with their peers in Singapore or the United States, and that English is the language they would need to tap into the rich resources of the internet. In parallel, the government launched a program to bring native speakers of English from the United States, Canada, the United Kingdom, and Australia to Georgia as volunteers. Their mission was, quite simply, to teach English to Georgia's English teachers, especially to help improve their practical language skills. The first wave of volunteers was small, but the program quickly became very popular. More and more families offered to house volunteers in their homes. The prospect of having a native speaker at the dinner table and being able to practice the language in everyday conversation was apparently very attractive. Particularly volunteers who were not only keen to tell locals about their own culture but were equally curious to learn about Georgian traditions proved very popular.

The experiment gathered momentum and became a big success. The third wave brought more than 2000 volunteers to Georgia. Every school in Georgia had at least one native speaker teaching English. The program was a key catalyst that helped establish English as a second language in

Georgia. Previously, Russian had been the dominant second language. Georgian students have to take one mandatory exam in one out of five foreign languages: Russian, English, German, French, or Spanish. Before the reform, only 35 percent of students chose English. In 2012, 75 percent chose English, and the results were encouraging: 72 percent of students passed at B1 level.[3]

That said, self-improvement can sometimes go awry despite a student's best intentions and initiative. As it happens, a friend of mine, Niko, a Georgian monk, was very eager to improve his English language skills, especially his conversational ability.

"I can read and I can write, but I don't speak well. I'm just not fluent in English," he said.

"Why don't you go abroad for a while, to an English-speaking country? That's what I did, and after a few months, I was fluent," another friend suggested.

That's what Niko did. He went online and found a monastery in the United Kingdom that accepted foreign visitors. He made arrangements for an extended stay by email.

Six months later, we met again.

"How's your English, Niko?", I asked him in English, but he didn't answer and tried to change the subject. This made me even more curious.

"Did you even go to the UK?", I asked, switching to Georgian.

"I did," he replied.

"What happened?"

"Well, I arrived in London. I took a bus, then another bus. The monastery was very hard to find, but eventually, I got there. But it turned out that all the monks there had taken a vow of silence. I ended up living in the UK for six months without hearing one word of English."

10.2 UNIVERSITY REFORM – FROM LENIN TO CLINTON

After the Rose Revolution, Georgia's tertiary education was in shambles. When Georgia was part of the Soviet empire, the focus was on Marxism, Leninism, and the history of the communist party. The only other area in which Georgian academics had some claim to excellence were natural sciences, such as physics, and mathematics. But all the best scientists had long left the country to take well-paid jobs abroad.

Many students were eager to study economics, but there was nobody who could have taught them. A few Marxists had tried to retrain themselves as international economists by reading *Economics: Principles, Problems, & Policies*, by Campbell McConnell and Stanley Brue, the only economics book of note that was available in Russian translation at the time. But they were obviously out of their element, incapable of teaching business studies, finance, or contract law to a generation of aspiring young people who had their minds set on Wall Street. In fact, many of the students were more familiar with McConnell & Brue than their lecturers.

10.2.1   *Degrees for Sale*

As a result of these shortcomings, corruption was the name of the game. The principal activity of Georgian academics in the mid-2000s was selling degrees to young people. This was, and partly still is, a prospering business that enriches heads of universities and departments, although their official salaries are in decline. This is because a university degree is almost obligatory as a status symbol in Georgia. Although this phenomenon is common in many other countries as well, it is especially pronounced in Georgia. It dates back to Soviet times, when being a university student would spare you the service in the Soviet army. Since Georgia was effectively occupied by the Soviet Union, the Soviet Army was perceived as a foreign force, and serving in it was perceived not as a service to Georgia. In fact, military service in the Soviet army was often a threat to a man's life because of the habitual brutalization of junior conscripts by their own commanders ("Dedovshchina," Russian for "reign of grandfathers"[4]). Because being a student offered some measure of protection from this cruel regime, Georgians became obsessed with academic credentials. The general perception was that a diploma was your only ticket to a good life, be it through a well-paid job or a rich spouse, and that young people who did not get a degree were a disgrace to their families. A university degree would also help you get promoted in a bureaucratic system that often relied on papers and stamps, rather than on merit and achievements. Because of the combined effect of these traditions and perceptions, universities made a fortune charging students for admission, good grades in end-of-year exams, and degrees. Preferential treatment in entrance exams was the most sought-after, and most costly service, which is why the centralization of these exams was such an important element of Georgia's education reform (see previous text).

10.2.2 *Partial Privatization and Scholarships*

While the centralization of entrance exams helped eradicate the biggest source of academic corruption, further attempts to reform Georgia's state-owned universities were less successful. Fresh blood should have been brought in by recruiting Georgian academics from abroad, but heads of universities and departments resisted such efforts in order to protect their staff from competition. In many ways, Georgia has not yet managed to reform its universities, much as it has largely failed to reform its justice system.

In other areas of tertiary education, however, Georgia made some progress. Some university facilities were privatized, and some new institutions offering higher education were launched, partly with financial support from the government. Today, almost 30 percent of all students in Georgia attend private universities, where the quality of education is much higher than at state-owned universities. This development encouraged many young people to study at the tertiary level.

To provide further encouragement, the government introduced scholarships for students who went abroad to pursue a master's degree. Any student admitted to one of the world's top 25 universities (according to rankings compiled by the *Financial Times* and *USA Today*) received a scholarship covering tuition, travel and accommodation. Acceptance into one of the top universities was the only criterion; the government did not require any additional assessments or exams. The program was open to students of engineering, natural sciences, and IT. In some years, business studies and law were also part of the program. The focus was on technical disciplines, because graduates in these fields were in short supply in Georgia at the time, and because the government perceived these subjects as the main drivers of Georgia's future economic development. Yet the scholarship itself was unconditional. It did not require graduates to come back and work for the Georgian government, or to come back to Georgia at all. When this aspect was publicized, the caliber of applicants improved significantly. The program was widely regarded as an important stepping stone on the way to a new, open-minded, hard-working elite that will eventually replace the communist intelligentsia in Georgia. Even if the country's tertiary education isn't yet fully reformed, a lot of young people are now highly motivated to study, work hard, and pursue a career that is based on merit, performance, and personal contribution, rather than on background, bribes, and connections.

10.2.3   Matching Skills to Vacancies

In the future, balancing the interests of students with the needs of the economy will be an important task for Georgia and countries in similar situations. Currently, the discrepancy between the skills of graduates and the requirements of the labor market is one of the biggest issues in tertiary education. Some studies say the number of unemployed people in the world roughly matches the number of vacancies at any given time. Many experts attribute this paradox to a mismatch of skills, although others contest this view.[5] In any case, the perceptions and attitudes of different stakeholders in tertiary education are anything but aligned. University graduates feel that what they learn at universities is not, or not sufficiently, relevant to their future success in the real world. The vast majority of university lecturers, however, is convinced that most of their graduates are ready to be employed, while potential employers argue that only one-third of all graduates fulfill the requirements of the job market. According to some studies, universities that work closely with the private sector have a much better success rate when it comes to post-graduation employment.

Unfortunately, only a few institutions take this problem seriously. These are typically the world's top-ranking universities whose reputation depends, at least to a certain degree, on the employability of their graduates. In contrast, most other universities pursue more self-centered objectives, such as admitting as many students as possible, or offering a wide range of partly exotic disciplines, many of which are not relevant from the perspective of potential employers. These universities are providers of degrees, rather than matchmakers between students and employers.

Should universities teach whatever students are interested in, or should their primary goal be to prepare future generations for a life of fulfilling and gainful employment? And do teenagers really know what they want, let alone what is best for them? There are no easy answers to these questions. But imagine, just for the sake of argument, that ancient mythology became hugely popular among teenagers for one reason or another, and that thousands of teenagers chose to study Greek and Roman mythology. Would the job market be able to absorb so many mythology experts? If it weren't, would universities not be acting irresponsibly by admitting so many applicants into this discipline in the first place?

Most universities are simply trying to make money, and they will offer whatever courses help them maximize their proceeds. If students demand mythology, and are willing to pay for it, universities will teach it, especially since many such exotic disciplines are much less costly to teach than, say, medicine or chemistry. An aspiring doctor needs a training hospital, and an aspiring chemist still needs a lab. In contrast, all a budding mythologist needs is a few books.[6] This applies even to state-funded universities, where students don't pay for tuition themselves, or at least not in full. As long as someone, be it an individual or the government, provides funds for every registered student, universities will continue to cater to the whims of applicants. Maybe there is a deficiency in this system, and perhaps tweaking university financing in a small way would help push the system toward a more efficient structure.

For example, the government could provide additional financing, e. g., in the shape of bonuses, to those universities whose graduates achieve the highest average employment rate. Alternatively, the government could introduce regulation that allows universities to charge students for services provided not only during their education, but also during the first few years of employment, based on their income. For instance, a certain percentage of the income tax graduates pay during the first two to three years after graduation could go directly to the university they graduated from. Such a system would help decrease tuition fees during the study period, when many students have little money to spare. What is more, it would increase the motivation of universities to find jobs for their graduates, be it by adjusting the number of places in a given discipline or by offering placement services for all those mythologists. Universities would work closely with potential employers to make sure their graduates have what it takes to succeed in the job market. During a transition period, the government could provide special financing to help prevent certain disciplines from dying out, even if graduates in these fields don't have the best employment prospects. This would help ensure that universities remain centers of culture and research. Certain institutions, such as arts colleges, musical conservatories, or pure research facilities, will require an altogether different financing formula. Compare the discussion in the previous chapter on healthcare facilities that are not commercially viable, but necessary to ensure comprehensive medical services for the population.

While such a structural reform of university financing has not yet been implemented in Georgia, it could be a game changer for tertiary education, both in Georgia and in other countries around the world.

10.2.4   An American University in Georgia

To help transform Georgia's tertiary education system, the government devised various lighthouse projects. Bringing an American university to Georgia was, perhaps, the most prominent of these projects. To establish an American university in Georgia, the government of Georgia signed a contract with the Millennium Challenge Corporation (MCC) a U.S. initiative that allocates grants to developing countries with a proven track record of promoting democracy and human rights. Almost all countries that have received these funds have spent them on infrastructure projects, such as roads, bridges, and water utilities, as Georgia had done with the first tranche of financing. But the government decided that the second tranche of the grant should be used to promote higher education – specifically, to establish an American university for technological studies in Georgia. Governments in other countries have pursued similar concepts in the past, but few of them have succeeded. The principal difference between this initiative and projects developed elsewhere is that this project is financed by the United States, not by funds derived from the exploitation of natural resources in the hosting state. A university based in the United States and selected through a tender process will be given sole responsibility for managing the university in Georgia. The government has no intention, nor will it be allowed, to intervene in any decision making. The degrees awarded by the American university in Georgia will be equivalent to those awarded by the parent institution in the United States. Effectively, the Georgian institution will be a satellite campus of the U.S. university. At the time of writing, the project is under development.

On a personal note, let me relate the story of how high-level support for this project was secured. That day, everybody was a bit nervous. People were running around, arranging and re-arranging chairs, tables, bottles of water, everything. We were expecting the U.S. Secretary of State Mrs. Hillary Clinton to discuss various aspects of Georgian-American relations: financial assistance, free trade, defense co-operation. My idea and my mission was to get Mrs. Clinton to green-light funding for tertiary education reform. At the time, Georgia had already received and spent a first tranche. Yet I was painfully aware that we were not succeding to reform the tertiary education system, one of my biggest personal regrets. The privatization of the Georgian Agrarian University and establishing of the Free Unversity (both by private investor – Kakha Bendukidze) were the only real success stories at the time. Establishing an American university in Georgia was a long shot, but I went for it anyway.

I was relieved to find that Mrs. Clinton was a much more genial person than you would think from seeing her on TV, that she was in a good mood, and that she clearly liked Georgia. My turn came and I pitched the idea of an American university in Georgia. I explained that, although I have a business degree myself, the focus should be on IT and engineering, the disciplines that I thought were most in need to develop Georgia's economy. Part of the funds from the MCC would be used to establish the university, while the rest would go to the best students in the form of scholarships. The university would be under U.S. management and award U.S. degrees.

"But there are some universities like this in the region, and some of them are not very successful," said Mrs. Clinton.

She was right, and I was prepared for her objection. I moved on to the next part of my presentation. I explained that the issue at these universities is the fact that the local government often meddles with decisions regarding staffing or the curriculum. In contrast, we would make the independence of the university's management an explicit condition of MCC financing to protect it from future attempts at interference.

"But do you think you will be able to attract a high-level U.S. university?"

This was her second question with negative connotation. One more – and the project would be dead. I admitted that a lot of U.S. universities were understandably afraid to take high risks in small, developing countries. But in this case, it would be different: a project led by the U.S. government and backed by U.S. financing, a one of a kind effort to bring Western excellence to a developing country. It would provide unparalleled opportunities to those who can least afford a good education, but who need it the most: the poor. It would be a fully merit-based enterprise. I made quite a speech. Everybody liked it. Our president nodded with satisfaction, and Mrs. Clinton looked like she was very much on board, especially after the last few sentences. We were all eagerly awaiting her verdict.

"But," she began.

I took a chance and interrupted her. If she finished this sentence, it would be over. I had run out of prepared arguments. I had to think up something new on the spot.

"Imagine, Madam Secretary," I started, not even knowing where I was going with this, "imagine a regional champion, a center for education and science, a center for scientific research and development. We still have some good scientists left in the region, and they are looking for a home. Not only Georgian students will be attending the American university. It will attract students from neighboring countries as well. Imagine, Madam Secretary, that, 20 years from now, the presidents of Armenia and Azerbaijan will have graduated from this University as classmates. Wouldn't that be something?"

Silence. She smiled and nodded. The project was approved a few months later. Georgia received a grant of USD 150 million.

NOTES

1. J.D. Salinger, *The Catcher in the Rye*, Little, Brown, and Company, New York, 1951 (Salinger 1951).
2. http://data.worldbank.org/indicator/SE.PRM.ENRL.TC.ZS/countries?page=1&display=default (retrieved in May 2016).
3. According to the Common European Framework of Reference for Languages, B1 is the third out of six levels of proficiency (A1 to C2). B1 is defined as follows: "Can understand the main points of clear standard input on familiar matters [...]. Can deal with most situations likely to arise whilst travelling in an area where the language is spoken. Can produce simple connected text and [...] describe experiences [...]." http://www.coe.int/t/dg4/linguistic/Source/Framework_EN.pdf (retrieved in May 2016).
4. https://www.hrw.org/reports/2004/russia1004/6.htm (retrieved in May 2016).

5. See Horst Entorf, *Mismatch Explanations of European Unemployment: A Critical Evaluation*, Springer Science & Business Media, 2012 (Entorf 2012).
6. In Germany, for example, a university education in medicine costs the government approximately EUR 200,000, more than 15 times the cost of an education in the humanities: http://www.saarbruecker-zeitung.de/alte_inhalte/universitaet-des-saarlandes/art298914, 3848035 (retrieved in May 2016).

CHAPTER 11

Formula for Leadership

Abstract This chapter presents Nika Gilauri's personal perspective on public leadership. He describes key success factors developed during his term as a leader in Georgia's reform government, initially as a cabinet member (from 2004, as minister of energy) and later as prime minister (2009–2012): a determined team, a shared vision, and decisive action. The chapter concludes with an account of crucial wartime leadership challenges during the Russian invasion of Georgia in 2008, including the story of how the author kept the country in cash with the help of a bottle of Jack Daniel's.

Keywords Leadership · Revolution · Team · Russia · war · George W. Bush

The transformation that took place in Georgia between 2004 and 2012 was more comprehensive, more substantial, and more sustainable than anyone would have hoped, especially in that part of the world. It is probably one of the finest examples of economic achievement in a small developing country in recent years, but the transformation went beyond economics. Despite many mistakes and setbacks, countries all over the world look to Georgia for inspiration because the results of lasting change for the better are clearly visible and widely recognized. The government that helped bring about this transformation relied on three principles: team, vision, and action.

© The Author(s) 2017   179
N. Gilauri, *Practical Economics*,
DOI 10.1007/978-3-319-45769-7_11

11.1   TEAM

Approach the government in some countries with a question, an issue, or a proposal, and nine out of ten times you will get the same answer, if you get an answer at all: "Sorry, not my remit." In Georgia's reform government, it was the exact opposite. No matter who – investors, entrepreneurs, citizens – came to any one of us, we made their concerns our own, regardless of whose department was formally responsible. We tackled every problem as a team, and every minister felt responsible for the government to succeed as a whole. Elsewhere, ministries are organizational silos, concerned only with their own performance. As a result, they often don't do anything, lest they be blamed when something goes wrong. And when something actually does go wrong, a minister's number one objective is typically to try and shift the blame to someone else. While our government wasn't entirely immune to this reflex, our creed was that we are one team, that we take decisions as a team, and that if anything goes wrong, we deal with it as a team. Internally, the constitutional bodies – the president, the prime minister, the cabinet, and the members of parliament – would argue a lot about every topic. But once a decision was made, we would all speak with one voice and do our best to see it through. There were two driving forces behind this attitude:

- *Collective appointment.* The cabinet was approved by the parliament as a whole, not minister by minister, as it is done in many other countries. In Georgia, it went as follows. The president was elected. Parliament was elected. The president presented a candidate for the prime minister to parliament, and the candidate presented a team and a program. Then parliament voted for, or against, the entire executive team and its program, not for or against individual ministers. This approach was adhered to even when there were changes in the cabinet. The prime minister could only replace up to 30 percent of the cabinet members, and four crucial ministries were exempt from the prime minister's discretion to begin with (interior, justice, defense, and penitentiary institutions). Once the admissible replacements were used up, the prime minister would have to seek a new mandate from parliament. Even the performance-based remuneration system was designed for the cabinet as a whole rather than for its individual members. Specifically, 50 percent of a minister's bonus was based on the performance of the country as a whole, as measured by the most comprehensive indicator, GDP growth.

- *Common mindset.* The members of the cabinet certainly disagreed and argued about a lot of political issues. Despite such disagreements, however, we shared a set of common values and attitudes. We were all in favor of democracy, meritocracy, and reform, inspired by and open to Western practices. We all felt that this was our one chance in life to do something for our country and make names for ourselves as men and women of action. Of course, it helped that we were all quite young when we were appointed. Nothing was sacred, and we were not afraid to try something new, or to fail. If we failed, we would try something else. There was a shared sense that innovation was a good thing, not a risk to be avoided.

Can other countries in need of reform replicate this spirit? I believe that they can. Many politicians complain that there is a lack of true talent in their countries, and that they have trouble attracting the best people to serve in the government or in state agencies. In my experience, the real problem is that politicians don't look beyond the usual suspects and hesitate to bring in new people. Of course, there is a limited number of good managers and daring innovators in any one party, or any one circle of people for that matter. The bold move that helped transform Georgia was to look for potential new team members all the time and everywhere. It does take guts, but it's not rocket science: find the most promising people, whoever they may be, and give them an opportunity to prove themselves. With this kind of approach, based on trial and error, you stand a much higher chance of creating a high-performing team than by thinking inside the box all the time. Of course, not every outsider will live up to the expectations, but over time, a new elite of civil servants will emerge. In Georgia, many heads of agencies and departments, and even many ministers and their deputies, were chosen not because of their affiliation with a party or a specific caste of people but because they had new ideas, felt strongly about particular topics, and were not afraid to speak their minds. In many cases, an appointment was made based on a simple conversation in which a candidate had impressed a cabinet member or an occasion on which a candidate had clearly excelled in the public eye. At one point, almost half the cabinet was not affiliated with any party. Even I, when serving as prime minister, was not a member of any party.

Another important characteristic of Georgia's reform government was its willingness to bring smart people into the team. Often, heads of organizations, agencies, ministries, or governments are afraid to appoint people they deem smarter than themselves as their subordinates, fearing that the new recruits will eventually challenge their authority or even make them redundant. The Georgian government that was in power from 2004 to 2012 had no such fear. Quite the opposite: ministers competed with one another to attract the smartest people to their staff, and they took pride in their teams. Cabinet members celebrated the accomplishments of their subordinates as if they were their own, an important source of motivation for junior staff members.

11.2   VISION

Few months after I took office as minister of energy in 2004, I asked my team to put together the calculations for a nationwide 24-hour electricity supply. I will never forget the puzzled looks on their faces.

"Why bother?", they asked. "You know as well as we do that Georgia will not have 24-hour electricity supply in our lifetime."

This was coming from the top specialists in the field, people who had worked in the energy sector for much longer than I had, and who knew the Georgian electricity system much better than I did at the time. Within 18 months of this conversation, 24-hour power supply had become a reality, and in 2007, we were exporting electricity to our neighbors. This experience taught me to see opportunity where others see nothing but obstacles. I made it my mission to inspire others to think that anything is possible, and that a vision can become a reality if the best people pull together to make it happen.

In 2004, nobody could imagine that Georgia would one day become a regional tourist hub, let alone one of the world's top tourist destinations. When President Saakashvili first proposed an investment program to develop the tourism infrastructure in Batumi, a port on the coast of the Black Sea, almost everybody was skeptical. Nobody believed that such an effort could possibly amount to anything. Back then, Georgia was widely considered unsafe for foreign visitors, a fundamental issue for any budding travel destination. There were unresolved geopolitical problems in our relations with Russia. Some territories were (and still are) occupied by the Russian army. There was also no tourism infrastructure to speak of. We did not have a single five-star hotel, and getting to Georgia was difficult even for those who were determined to try. What is more, Georgia was facing fierce competition from top tourist destinations in the region, countries like Turkey and Greece. These countries have a well-established reputation among vacationers worldwide, world-class infrastructure, world-class connectivity, and milder climates affording longer tourism seasons. It took a grand vision, an enormous effort, and tremendous team-work to make it happen, but it did happen. As early as 2011, *Monocle* magazine proclaimed a "Batumi Boom" and reported that "Georgia's second city is in the midst of a frantic transformation from sleepy resort to major tourist and investment hub."[1] The number of visitors to Georgia increased from 350,000 in 2004 to five million in 2012.

Had someone floated the idea of building a defense industry in Georgia in the mid-2000s, any expert in the field would have taken it for a joke and laughed out loud. At the time of writing, Georgia is not only producing equipment for its own defense systems but also exporting defense tech-nology to other countries.[2]

The most important vision, however, was not tied to any sector or industry, be it energy, tourism, or defense. Rather, the big vision was that all stakeholders in the country – the population, investors, local businessmen, and civil servants – would rally around and work toward a common goal: building a better Georgia – a country that is free of corruption, has a highly efficient government, and acts as a hub in its region. A country in which poverty is a thing of the past and in which hard work will earn you a decent living. Mistakes were made along the way, and the transformation is not yet complete, but this is certainly not due to a lack of vision.

11.3   Action

The reform government was all about action and accountability. We took decisions as a team and saw them through as individuals who share the same set of values. The setup of the government and its procedures were specifically designed to support this approach. Even if some deci-sions were effectively made by individual ministers, the final and formal decision was mostly approved by the cabinet as a whole. There was a special committee for every major topic, comprising the relevant min-isters, members of parliament, directors of state-owned companies and agencies, heads of relevant regulators, and experts in the field. Committee sessions were chaired by the prime minister. In-depth dis-cussions about the development of a particular sector (be it energy, telecommunications, road infrastructure, or education) took place in these committees. Objectives and concrete steps to achieve these objectives were defined there, and the committees drafted decision proposals for the government. The cabinet convened every week and took decisions collectively by vote. The purpose of this collective voting was to make sure that every cabinet member was aware of what was going on and would back the outcome, no matter how complex the process leading up to the decision might have been. At the same time, one person, and one person only, was responsible for following up each decision and overseeing its implementation. Whenever two or more people were named as the responsible parties, conflicts or delays arose. This is why we combined collective decision making with individual responsibility for implementation. It helped us take bold decisions and ensure fast action.

Acting fast is also what helped Georgia cope with crises, and Georgia faced more crises over the course of a few years than some countries face throughout their entire history. Over time, crisis management became second nature to the government. Specifically, the team-based fast action approach helped Georgia survive various regional crises, such as the one in Ajara in 2004,[3] the energy crisis in 2006,[4] the world economic crisis that started in 2007 and hit Georgia in the midst of a home-grown political turmoil and an outflow of foreign capital; political crises, such as the blocking of the whole center of Tbilisi by the opposition in 2010;[5] and the biggest crisis of all, the Russian invasion in August 2008.

11.4 THE RUSSIAN INVASION

In August, 2008, Russian tanks started rolling into the Tskhinvali region. On August 12, 2008, the Security Council – most members of the government and some members of parliament – had gathered in President Mikheil Saakashvili's office. The Russian army was only about ten kilometers from Tbilisi and still advancing. None of us had slept in days. We were tired but full of energy and determination.

We were discussing the next steps. At the time, I was minister of finance and first deputy prime minister. All major roads, railroads, and points of entry had already been blocked. By cutting off all supplies, the Russians might try to get the Georgian population to rise up against their own elected government.

"Okay, we need to decide on a few things," said Prime Minister Lado Gurgenidze.

"I will reach out to all the investors and all foreigners who have been doing any kind of business with Georgia," he announced. As a former banker, Lado was very good at "selling" the country, even in difficult moments like this one.

"The president, the minister of foreign affairs, and the Security Council are in talks with the international media and foreign politicians – Americans, Europeans, and so on," he continued, "but we need some-body in charge of the economy, someone who will take care of the day-to-day economic affairs of the country, to make sure we get all the necessary supplies." There was silence.

"I propose that Eastern Georgia should be managed by Nika Gilauri," said the prime minister. Silence. Nobody agreed, nobody disagreed. I realized that I had a huge job to do, and that I should have left right away to get started. But I wanted to hear who my counterpart for Western Georgia would be, so that we would be able to coordinate our actions. I lingered for a few more minutes.

"Well, if there are no other candidates, then I guess Nika should be in charge of supplies for all of Georgia," Lado said and looked at me. What was there to say? I nodded, got up, explained that I had a lot to do, and said my goodbyes. It wasn't the first time that I was given a job nobody else wanted, simply because nobody could conceive how it was supposed to be done.

I rushed to my office. During the short drive, I thought about the tasks at hand. I would have to provide food, water, drugs, electricity, gas, petrol, and cash to a country invaded by 100,000 Russian soldiers and who knows how many tanks. There were Russian air strikes every day. The Russian army had taken control of most of the country's crucial infrastructure, including the port of Poti and the Georgian railway, and was moving toward Tbilisi. When I got to my office, I asked my team to gather all economic and social ministers right away. My office staff told me later that this was the first time I had a crazy look on my face. It was not surprising – this was the first time I had no clue what to do.

I needed a plan. I needed a team. Instead, I found myself surrounded by a group of ministers who had no idea what to do either. They were all looking at me expectantly. This was when I realized that I couldn't let my own perplexity show. If they saw me acting lost, or as if I didn't know what I was doing, we would fail miserably. I mustered all my strength and convinced myself that I knew exactly what needed to be done. I started explaining my action plan. I could hardly believe my own words. A minute earlier, I had had no idea where even to start, let alone what my concrete action plan would be.

"Where danger threatens, salvation also grows," as Friedrich Hölderlin put it.[6] Within one hour, we had an action plan. Initially, we focused on food. We had identified the twelve types of food that were most widely consumed: bread, cheese, butter, wheat, beef, poultry, milk, and so on. Monitoring this basket of essential products would alert us to imminent shortages. We tracked the prices of these products three times a day in Georgia's ten largest cities, including the capital and regional centers. In each city, we picked a handful of shops. We instructed three different government agencies to monitor the prices of each product type and send the information to my office. The representative of the local government was in charge of monitoring the prices in the morning, the department of statistics did the same thing in the afternoon, and the revenue service took over the evening shift. We had purposefully split the job between three agencies to ensure some measure of checks and balances. Everybody was nervous during these difficult days. Occasionally, local governors called us in a panic, claiming that their region was out of food and demanding that we send them additional supplies. Thanks to our triple sources, we knew that these claims were usually false. As soon as the price of one of the products in a particular region went up, we sent additional supplies of that product to the region. We didn't, however, give these supplies away for free but sold them to the local shops to make sure the regions received only what they really needed. This system helped us avoid any shortage of essential food products during the war.

Demand management was under control. Our next task was supply management. Where would we find the products we needed, and how would we get them to the regions? The Russian army had blocked both the railway and the main East-West highway. This is why we established two bases, one in Eastern Georgia and one in Western Georgia, each stocking the twelve essential food products. To stock the bases, we bought products from wholesalers, rather than from shops. This was to make sure there were no empty shelves in shops, which might have caused a panic among the population. In fact, we didn't even buy everything the wholesalers were offering. We left them with enough supplies to keep stocking shops in Tbilisi and in large cities.

I was relieved that our improvised system of price control was working. There was no shortage of any of the essential products and nobody panicked. Nobody even skipped a line in a supermarket, and nobody broke any traffic rules. The fact that the people of Georgia were so law-abiding, so supportive of each other, and so calm despite the invasion made me incredibly proud of my country. Still, that whole period is very much a blur to me. Our days started at 7 am in the morning and ended at 4 am the next morning. We went through prices, took stock of supplies, and arranged for deliveries. Based on our intelligence about the movements of the Russian army, we tried to anticipate where our citizens might take refuge and arranged to have food supplies waiting for them.

When food supplies started to run low at wholesalers' warehouses, we started importing food supplies ourselves. We rented a few warehouses around Tbilisi and near Batumi to store our imports. We bought supplies for Western Georgia from Turkey and for Eastern Georgia from Azerbaijan. As it happened, one of my fellow ministers, Alexander "Ale" Khetaguri, the minister of energy, had been on an official visit in Azerbaijan when the Russians invaded Georgia. I asked him to stay in Baku to help manage the imports. Every day, I received a report about the stock of supplies in our warehouses. Based on this information, we imported additional goods from Turkey and Azerbaijan.

There were even some cases of wartime heroism behind the lines. Quite understandably, some drivers had refused to drive trucks loaded with supplies through territory that was controlled by the Russians. In those cases, employees of the revenue service got behind the wheel themselves and drove the vehicles past the posts of the Russian army. In another case, we had to build a tent city to provide shelter for thousands of internally displaced persons from the Tskhinvali region. We had the necessary materials and we had a suitable site, but we had no manpower to put up the tents. Most members of the army and the police were at the front line. I called on the members of parliament to help out. In less than an hour, they were on site, with their friends and families, and rolled up their sleeves. By the next morning, the tent city was ready. It housed thousands of internally displaced persons – women and men, children and old people, newborn babies and pregnant women. Volunteers delivered bread and sausages several times a day to feed them.

Thanks to determined leadership, good crisis management, and the tenacity of the Georgian people, Tbilisi did not fall in 2008. The population did not take to the streets to demand the resignation of the elected government, despite the Russians' best efforts to starve the capital and stir up an insurgence.

11.5   TRADING JACK FOR BENJAMIN

In the midst of the invasion, I got a call from the National Bank.

"Nika, we are out of cash."

"What do you mean, you are out of cash? You are the National Bank. You have more than enough reserves."

"No, you don't understand. We have more than enough reserves, but these are all in accounts. What we don't have enough of is actual bills. The banks are running out of actual bank notes. Everybody is withdrawing US dollars and euros from ATMs. If we don't fill up the cash machines, they will run out in two days. We need to bring in cash from abroad."

"From where?"

"From Austria. We have already talked to them. Everything is ready. But how do we get the bills into Georgia?"

"How much are we talking about?"

"Around 350 million US dollars."

"Okay. I will take care of the logistics."

I tried to exude confidence, but in reality, I had no idea how to pull it off. Almost all flights to Georgia had been cancelled. Every plane entering Georgian airspace would be escorted by a Russian fighter jet. I pictured a cargo plane full of cash shot down by the Russians, showering us with Benjamins.[7] Putting it all on a single plane was too big a risk. We would have to hedge our bets. I rang up the Georgia Air Company and asked them to send a plane to Vienna to pick up USD 100 million to cover the immediate need. I decided to have the rest flown to Azerbaijan and brought to Georgia by land, a much safer option. Ideally, we would have brought in the entire amount that way, but we needed the first USD 100 million the next day. Going through Azerbaijan would take much longer. To buy us some time, we announced an ad hoc bank holiday.

When the plane from Vienna finally landed at Tbilisi airport, I was there with an escort of eight special operations soldiers. I hadn't told anyone where we were going, or what we were transporting. Driving around a war zone with USD 100 million in cash is, well, a little risky to begin with, but telling people about it would have turned the operation into a downright suicide mission. As it happened, we delivered the package safely to the vault of the National Bank. I instructed the banks to re-open earlier than usual the next day to show everyone that there was no shortage of cash. The main concern was to avoid that lines of people would snake out of the banks. The banks managed it well. Some banks even gave cash to their employees and had them deposit it in their accounts for everyone to see, saying that they had withdrawn it that morning, that there was no issue with the supply, and that their money would be safer in their accounts than in their homes. By the end of that day, people started bringing back cash and depositing it in their accounts. The crisis was averted. Not one request by international depositor or investor was delayed for a minute.

I turned my attention to the remaining USD 250 million. I had the cash flown to Baku, Azerbaijan. Ale, Georgia's minister of energy, was still in Baku at the time. I called him on a secure line at the Georgian Embassy there and briefed him on the situation. I asked him to pick up the cash at Baku airport and bring it to the Azeri-Georgian border where I would meet him.

"Ale, listen carefully. When you leave the embassy, you will not have access to a secure line. So when you call me from your mobile, don't mention the money. Let's call it the guest. When you tell me that the guest has arrived, I will know that you have the cash. When you tell me that the guest is feeling well, I will know that you have counted the cash and it is all there. I may not be able to make it to the border in time because of the traffic.[8] In that case, I will tell you to 'fuck off', and you will store the cash in a safe place in Baku. If, however, I tell you to 'get lost', you will bring the cash to the border. Understood?"

"Understood. But 'fuck off' and 'get lost' sound so similar. We might get confused. Can't we use a different code?"

"I'm not feeling particularly creative right now, and there's no time. Let's stick with these phrases. Let's write down what they mean."

"Ok. I will call you in a few hours. But I have one request."

"What is it?"

At this point, I was prepared for pretty much anything, but Ale's answer still took me by surprise.

"You know how much I love Jack Daniel's."

"So?"

"I keep a bottle in my office. It was a gift from the US ambassador. When you come to the border, can you please bring me the bottle?"

"I'll tell you what. You bring me USD 250 million, and I will bring you the bottle. That's going to be the most expensive bottle of whiskey in the world."

We hung up. My phone rang a few hours later. I was on my way to the border. As I had feared it was almost impossible to get to the Azeri border.

"Nika, our guest has arrived."

"Is he feeling well?"

"Yes, he is ok. What shall we do?"

"Fuck off."

"Wait. Fuck off?"

I checked my notes.

"Yes, fuck off."

There was silence on the line. I realized that Ale, too, was looking at his notes.

"Ok. We will fuck off."

After a few hours, traffic had eased. I would finally be able to get to the border without further delays. Again, I could not tell anyone where I was going, or what my mission was. I was accompanied by the same team of special operations soldiers that had protected the pick-up at the airport. We were in two armored vehicles. To this day, there are allegations in

Georgia that these vehicles carried members of the Georgian government trying to flee to Azerbaijan. But in fact, it was me on my way to trade a bottle of Jack for a truckload of Benjamins. I called Ale on his mobile.

"Ale, you can get lost now."

"What? Get lost? Wait, which one is that? So, get lost?"

"Yes, get lost."

"Okay."

A little later, I was in the neutral territory between the Georgian and Azeri borders, surrounded by handful special operations soldiers, holding a bottle of Jack Daniel's Tennessee Whiskey in my hand. It was pitch dark. I couldn't see a thing. I heard footsteps.

"Ale, is that you?"

"Who do you think?"

"Thank God."

Ale stepped into the light.

"Where is my whiskey?"

"I've got it right here."

I showed him the bottle and started moving toward him.

"Where is my money?"

"I've got it right here."

An armored truck inched forward into the light.

"Do you want to count it?"

"Have you counted it?"

"I have. It's all there."

"Okay. Here's your whiskey."

I passed him the bottle of Jack Daniel's. We said our goodbyes. I headed back to Tbilisi with USD 250 million in cash, and Ale headed back to Baku to help arrange for further food supplies to be brought into Georgia.

A few days later, George W. Bush announced that the United States would send humanitarian aid to Georgia, and that he had charged the navy with delivering it ("Operation Assured Delivery"[9]). On September 8, 2008, the USS Mount Whitney, the flagship of the 6th U.S. Fleet, arrived in Georgia, carrying tons of aid and thousands of soldiers. The war was over.

11.6   THE WAR ROOM

A few days later, a high-ranking U.S. general asked me where I had received my wartime logistics training.

"It was an on-the-job training program. It started on August 8. I can't say that I like it, but I'm definitely learning a lot about crisis management."

The general smiled and asked whether he could see our war room.

"I was told that you are in charge of the war room, providing food supplies to the population. If it is not confidential, may I see it?"

"Of course," I said. I think he expected to see a sophisticated underground facility, with lots of computer screens and the latest communication technology. I took him to the war room – my office. A few tired-looking ministers were gathered there. One of them was taking a power nap on my couch. The strategic equipment consisted of a handful of mobile phones, a whiteboard filled with various calculations, and a large wall map of Georgia with markings that indicated the emplacements of the Russians and destinations for our food deliveries. For a second, the general looked at me with a frown, as if I was pulling his leg and hiding the true war room from him. But then he looked at our faces and realized that this was really it.

"May my assistant take a photo of the room?", he asked.

"Be my guest," I said.

I wonder whether that photo still exists.

NOTES

1. https://monocle.com/magazine/issues/48/batumi-boom/ (retrieved in May 2016).
2. http://georgiatoday.ge/news/3396/Georgian-Delta-to-Increase-Export-to-GEL-300-Million (retrieved in May 2016).

3. http://www.crisisgroup.org/en/regions/europe/south-caucasus/geor gia/b034-saakashvilis-ajara-success-repeatable-elsewhere-in-georgia.aspx (retrieved in May 2016).
4. Russia blew up two gas pipelines leading into the country and a high-voltage electricity line simultaneously on the coldest winter day in 2006. See http://news.bbc.co.uk/2/hi/europe/4637034.stm (retrieved in May 2016).
5. http://eng.kavkaz-uzel.ru/articles/13178/ (retrieved in May 2016).
6. *Patmos*, by Friedrich Hölderlin (1803, first printed in 1807 in *Musen almanach*). English translation taken from Anselm Haverkamp, *Leaves of Mourning: Hölderlin's Late Work*, New York, SUNY Press, 1996, p. 48 (Haverkamp 1996).
7. "Benjamin" is a slang expression for the hundred dollar bill, referring to the portrait of Benjamin Franklin. See http://www.urbandictionary.com/define.php?term=Benjamin&defid=1384165 (retrieved in June 2016).
8. Many people were leaving the country, causing a traffic jam at the border between Georgia and Azerbaijan.
9. http://www.navy.mil/submit/display.asp?story_id=39560 (retrieved in May 2016).

AFTERWORD – FROM PLUTOCRACY TO MERITOCRACY

The idea of this book is not only to tell the true story of an incredible economic transformation and government reforms that took place in Georgia in 2004–2012, but also to provide some analyses of the reasons behind the success stories and failures and to try and systemize the results while reaching as broad an audience as possible. The end result is – based on Georgian example and examples of many countries that have been studied – that none of the existing economic theories are applicable and that a practical approach is needed to every concrete reform in every single country. Copying and pasting does not work – but learning from others' experience and innovating to adopt to local realities is the formula for success.

Practical Economics was the basis for the Georgian success story – looking at every problem, every reform from many different angles (private sector's, citizens', international investors', budgetary as well as regulatory angles), analyzing it based on international experience and adopting for local realities, thinking outside of box, innovating, and solving each problem in that particular context. These are the main characteristics of Practical Economics. However, this approach (much easier said than implemented) would not have been possible to practice if there had not been "open access" of the government, inclusiveness of the institutions, and a major mindset shift from plutocracy to meritocracy.

In the book *Why Nations Fail*, the authors D. Acemoglu and J. Robinson argue that "countries differ in their economic success because

© The Author(s) 2017
N. Gilauri, *Practical Economics*,
DOI 10.1007/978-3-319-45769-7

of their different institutions, the rules influencing how the economy works, and the incentives that motivate people." They argue that there are inclusive and extractive institutions – the first ones are based on meritocracy, on private property, rule of law, and public services that provide a level playfield for all. The latter is characterized by the opposite features.

When looking back at the 2004–2012 period and assessing the successes and failures of that time, I truly believe that one of the main factors of the incredible turnaround story and one of the main ingredients of the success formula was an incredible shift from plutocracy to meritocracy. Maybe it was not enough to create comprehensive, across-the-border inclusive institutions but some major characteristics were there. Maybe this period was not enough to introduce fully functioning rule of law or private property aspects of the inclusive institutions, but meritocracy and public services were definitely big achievements that laid the groundwork of economic success and mindset shift that have been described in this book.

Communist regime was based on full-blown extractive institutions – where there was no rule of law, no meritocracy, no freedom of people to choose what they wanted to do – where you could not get promoted if you were not a member of Communist Party (the only party that existed in the Soviet Union) and where the elite of the Communist Party were the only source of power; where only the elite of the Communist Party with one phone call could help you become a student of any university or promote you to any position, or even save you from any trouble with the law, or help you in the court room. And if you were not part of this elite circle, it did not matter how hard working, smart, intelligent, or innovative you were, there was not much you could do about your future or about your family.

Unfortunately, when the Soviet Union broke down Georgia continued to live with the same rules. The power of the elite – to take decisions like who gets promoted and who does not, who gets to go to university and who does not, or sometimes even showing kindness and choosing a poor relative from a countryside and helping him/her to go through life – was all too sweet to let go. Bringing Shevardnadze from Moscow and supporting him throughout 1990s and early 2000s was nothing else but the wish of the ex-communist elite to continue with the same lifestyle as during the Soviet Union. The closed system was the main reason for the failed country that Georgia had become in early 2000s and open access was the main characteristic of Georgia's turn-around during 2004–2012. The most important messages that were sent to the society after the Rose Revolution were by introducing free and fair university admission exams – where anybody could become a student of any university based only on their skills and knowledge; by accepting at the highest government positions people that were not members of any party; and by promoting public employees based on their achievements rather than on their personal relations with anybody. These messages gave a hope to everyone that anything was possible, gave a hope to everyone to "pursue happiness" and motivated everyone to work, to study to be dedicated, which as a result created the drive, the buzz, the environment that is a formula for success and for growth.

Freedom, open access, and meritocracy were the key characteristics of the transformation that contributed the most to the incredible transformation story of Georgia.

References

Entorf, Horst. 2012. *Mismatch Explanations of European Unemployment: A Critical Evaluation.* Berlin: Springer Science & Business Media.

Hanke, Steve H., Alexander B. Rose, and Stephen J.K. Walters, *How* to make medicine safe and *cheap*, Health and Medicine, Fall 2014.

Haverkamp, Anselm. 1996. *Leaves of Mourning: Hölderlin's Late Work*, 48. New York: SUNY Press.

Jones, Stephen F. 2014. The Making of Modern Georgia, 108. London/New York: Routledge. http://pdf.usaid.gov/pdf_docs/Pdacn591.pdf. Retrieved in May 2016.

Kuttner, Robert. 2013. *Debtors' Prison: The Politics of Austerity versus Possibility.* New York: Knopf.

New York Times. Roses and Reality in Georgia, *New York Times*, November 10, 2007, http://www.nytimes.com/2007/11/10/opinion/10sat3.html (retrieved in 2015).

Onishi, Norimitsu, Be Polite or Else, Giuliani Warns in Announcing Civility Campaign, *New York Times*, February 26, 1998.

Osterweil, Willie, The Secret Shopper, *The New Enquiry*, June 4, 2012.

Salinger, J.D. 1951. *The Catcher in the Rye.* New York: Little, Brown, and Company.

Seddon, Max and Neil Buckley, Russia: Magnitsky's bitter legacy, *Financial Times*, June 12, 2016.

Spiegel, Uriel and Joseph Templeman. 2004. A Non-Singular Peaked Laffer Curve: Debunking the Traditional Laffer Curve. *The American Economist* 48(2) Fall: 61–66.

INDEX

© The Author(s) 2017
N. Gilauri, *Practical Economics*,
DOI 10.1007/978-3-319-45769-7

Printed by Printforce, the Netherlands